Journey Toward Poetry

Jean Burden

JOURNEY TOWARD POETRY

October House Inc New York

Seven of these chapters (somewhat modified from their
original form) have already appeared as articles in:
Ante, Author & Journalist, Mademoiselle, Trace, Yankee.

Published by October House Inc.
134 East 22nd Street, New York

Library of Congress catalog card number

Printed by Clarke & Way, Inc., New York, U.S.A.

Table of Contents

Preface by the Author

THIS IS essentially a book in the first person singular. It is in no sense a scholarly book, but it is a professional one. A journey toward any art is perforce a journey one takes alone, and solitary travels are, I think, the only kind worth describing.

Almost all poets are also involved to some degree with both the teaching and criticism of poetry. We conduct workshops, write reviews, edit manuscripts, conduct columns in magazines. This book is about all these related activities—written, not on a level of abstract theory, but from a highly personal, if roving, viewpoint.

It is not a book of rules for writing poetry, conducting a seminar, or editing a Poetry Page. It is rather a book of non-rules, a personal witness to the problems and possibilities of the creative imagination. It is not a book one may consume like a magic wafer and thereby be turned—presto—into a poet. It is, hopefully, a book to turn to for signs of what is genuine, difficult, and worth caring about in this art form. It is not just about craft. It is a book that I hope may point a way, encourage, enlighten—even entertain—both those who write poetry and those who read it. It is not a handbook in the usual sense; it is a small, meaningful, and sometimes humorous testament of a journey and a way.

Journey Toward Poetry

Prologue: Woman as Artist

I ONCE OVERHEARD at Steuben's a remark that probably could only be possible in this country, and in this era. Said one mother to another, "The trouble with Janey is that all her gifts are creative!"

A clinical psychologist for a California school district stated flatly the other day that the greatest discrimination in our society today is not against racial minorities, but against the gifted child and, particularly, the gifted girl.

A twelve-year-old who had already shown striking evidence of a talent for sculpture asked her mother whether, when she grew up, she had to get married. "I'd rather be an artist than a wife, and I don't think I can be *both*." (Only her father was upset by the question.)

These three instances—out of many that could be cited—point up a few aspects of a highly complicated problem that begins in childhood but gets no easier with time. And while the over-all problem is common to both sexes, it is the feminine side of it which is undoubtedly the more acute.

In brief, how does the woman who is *au fond* a creative artist live out her creativity, while at the same time fulfilling her biological and traditional roles as wife and mother?

The question is related to, but not the same as, the much older question of the equality of women, the "battle of the sexes," and the emancipation of woman from the kitchen. As a woman writer, I myself feel neither imprisoned nor embattled by the opposite sex. The problem, it seems to me, lies more in another area, and it is this I wish to explore, even if briefly.

In other words, it seems to me there is a new kind of suffrage at work, another kind of emancipation, not only for women as such, but for the small but infinitely important minority of women artists. And here we do not mean, of course, the dabblers, the women of small talent who are satisfied with "hobbies," but the genuinely gifted women who were born with talent of respectable size and who have a responsibility to it. Within such as these there breeds a far greater conflict than ever existed between man and woman, and few of either sex fully understand the *nature of the tension*, let alone what to do about it.

The problem has in no sense been invented for the sake of this essay. One has only to listen to the spirited conversations between women writers or women of other and various artistic endeavors or, better yet, to overhear their oftentimes futile attempts to explain their predicament to men. As a writer, I am in their company often. Sometimes we are a closed group, and then the frustration is fairly candid. Other times we are with husbands and children, and the itch and discomfort are much more veiled. Women artists have a hard enough time being frank with each other —not out of duplicity but often out of ignorance of what is really pushing them around—but they are usually awkward and tongue-tied when trying to explain themselves to men. Many of them, for this reason and for others, have fled to psychiatrists. What are they really seeking? A justification for their ego-expressions? Some of their critics have accused them of this. I think the answer is more subtle.

The sense of alienation that the creative minority—from the gifted child to the adult woman artist—feels is not just her isolation from the "crowd" (this can often be more welcome than distasteful). Nor does it arise from hostility from men, though the hostility is often real. It springs, in my opinion, from the struggle *between the masculine and feminine aspects of her own nature* and her total ignorance that these polarities even exist. She is driven by a masculine drive as well as feminine; she must live out both sides of her nature.

The premise on which this statement is based is not original with me. Virginia Woolf knew it well. Perhaps, she thought, there are "two sexes in the mind corresponding to the two sexes in the body"; perhaps they "also require to be united in order to get complete satisfaction and happiness." Coleridge, too, thought that a purely masculine or purely feminine mind might not be able to create.

Let me state the theory again, simply: *The artist is essentially androgynous, psychologically*. It is from this polarity between her masculine and feminine natures that woman creates.

Within those wholly, or almost wholly, oriented to their own biological gender this conflict (and this agonizing creativity) does not exist. The wholly male male and completely female female do not have this problem. They live within their male and female selves with none of this *type* of conflict. Prototypes: the aggressive, outgoing, dominating

5

male; and the passive, domesticated, all-wrapped-up-in-children female.

It does not take much analogizing to see that the creative act in art is essentially an expression of a masculine drive. It is not passive; it is an aggressive action. I recall discussing this with the late Thomas Sugrue and hearing him say, "Whenever I write a poem I have to gather myself into the masculine side of me, and *thrust* into the feminine side. The result is a poem." And the same analogy of course applies to the opposite sex.

It occurs whenever a woman puts paint on canvas, composes a sonata, conceives a ballet, writes a novel, or chips out a piece of sculpture from the granite of her own imagination. This is one way she can live out her *animus*, her own masculine self, and it is ignorance to say that this self does not exist, or only exists in the neurotic woman.

The word "animus," while made popular by C. G. Jung, was not original with him. Novelists Rider Haggard and Thomas Hardy, for example, were quite familiar with it, and with its counterpart, "anima," the feminine nature of man. It was Jung who made convincing through his case histories (and particularly his research into dreams) the premise that each sex carries the homologues of the other, and that both male and female have a difficult time recognizing the characteristics of their own sex in the opposite.

If this is true, how is it manifested in modern woman? Let us take first the large body of women who are not "anima-type" women, but who are not artists. How do they live out this "man" within them, this animus? Sometimes, of course, it is ignored completely, with frequently resulting distortions of personality, neuroses, etc. Often, for better or worse, it propels her into a career. Perhaps it sends her back to college when her children are all in school; it may even suggest she go into public life in a small way (or sometimes in a large way), as a friend of mine has recently done who became a delegate of her political party to the state convention. These solutions—and others like them—will work to the degree that the woman herself understands what is driving her—that she is not *competing* with men, but living out her latent side in order not only to prove it exists but finally to gather it into her larger, and more productive, individuality.

If the values of her animus, however, are projected to the world in a work of art—which is the subject at hand here —we have a similar but greater problem. For to these women art is not a sublimation of some frustrated sex urge —contrary to what many suppose—but a *primary drive* to which all others, however urgent, are never superior, and indeed, are often secondary. "I am a *writing animal*," says a prolific author of children's stories. "I can't remember when I didn't paint," says a portrait painter, and wife of a career diplomat. "I've been composing songs as long as I can remember," testifies another woman. "How long have you been writing?" I am frequently asked. "I can't remember," I have to reply vaguely. "Always, I guess." In other words, art is one vitally important way we women must experience life.

That it is not the *only* way makes for trouble. If it were, a woman could live alone, pursue her own ends, and live out her talent or her genius unhampered by other responsibilities. Many do just that, never daring to link their lives with another for fear of diluting the intensity of their drive, of sidetracking their primary purpose.

Some have tried marriage only to find their husbands either jealous of their art or unable to accept its demands on them. They have returned to single life, often finding it as blessed as the old aphorism promised. ("Are you really happy?" I am often asked. And I can reply honestly, "Not always with my circumstances, certainly. But with myself, yes.")

But what of those women artists who demand of life the full expression of both their feminine and masculine "souls"? We are back with our original question: *How does the woman who is, au fond, a creative artist live out her creativity, while at the same time fulfilling her biological and traditional roles as wife and mother?*

7

In the not too distant past, of course, she was not even allowed to ask the question. Almost all fields of artistic achievement were locked tight against her, and the few that were open did not permit her to enter on an equal footing with men. Women weren't allowed on the stage until the 17th century, and most of them could neither read nor write. When they finally dared to express themselves in novels (in the 19th century) they sent their manuscripts to publishers under a man's name.

The conflicts which the modern woman artist experiences are not these, but they are just as real. She is obviously pulled in two directions at once. All kinds of practical problems handicap her. How, primarily, does she find *time* to be both mother-wife and artist? Where does she gather enough *energy* to write a novel and drive Junior back and forth to school, keep house, cook three meals a day, shop for groceries, meet the commuters' train, entertain, and share in her husband's life? The conflict with which all artists are faced—the need for solitude and the equally profound need to mix in the world—is in her exaggerated and heightened, sometimes unbearably. How can she carve out of her days enough opportunity, not just to paint or write or whatever, but to *think* about it? "It is getting harder and harder just to find time to brood," a novelist friend of mine complains. Her children are grown, her husband is a prominent civic leader, she has plenty of means so that servants and a secretary carry a good portion of the drudgery of existence. But she still has to fight for solitude against the demands of an active and important public life. "I am sometimes torn to pieces," she confesses. "You see, I love both aspects of my life. Both are terribly important!" It is all very well to say she must make a choice. That is too easy an answer. How is she going to choose between a husband she adores, a gracious and beautiful way of life to which she contributes a great deal, and the exacting disciplines and joys of her creative life? Wealth and position may be more of a handicap than a blessing, though the woman artist who must grub for a living eight hours a day in an office, squeezing all

8

her creativity into weekends, may find this difficult to believe.

Another friend who had turned an old barn into a studio at some distance from the house was making a fair success at solving the problem of how to be a landscape painter and a wife and mother. She spent every morning in her studio and many afternoons walking over the countryside, sketching. When the family went to New England for a holiday, she would take her sketch pad with her and make notes while the others sailed or hiked. Always rather shy and ungregarious, she was content that their social life was, for the most part, restricted to small dinners with friends. All this harmony was disrupted when her husband was appointed to an important government position which necessitated moving to a busy city and almost constant socializing. "I try to sketch what I see from these windows," she told me, "but I miss the trees and the light on the meadow. All I see is gray here. Worst of all, I have nothing to say to these people."

Another woman, a dancer, solved her problem, but rather drastically, first by refusing to have children, and second, by effecting an amiable separation from her husband after fifteen years of happy marriage. She maintains her career in one city; he carries on an equally successful one a hundred miles away in the country, and they meet on occasional weekends. Each admires the other tremendously, and neither would ever contemplate divorce. But this, admittedly, is an exceptional instance.

A less radical solution is one found by a novelist whose children are away at school and whose husband is a sports enthusiast. Instead of feeling put upon by this arrangement, she welcomes her weekends free of responsibilities and is ready with dinner and conversation when her spouse returns from his game. The result of having seven days a week at her disposal (and boundless energy, I am compelled to add!) has meant that she has turned out more books than most people could accomplish in twice the time. Furthermore, her husband is as proud of her and as interested in her work as her most devoted friend—which of course he also is.

This brings into focus an important point: the problem of the woman artist is considerably less acute when her husband is sympathetic with it. It is astonishing how seldom this is true. Are there really so few men sufficiently secure in their masculinity that they do not feel threatened by their wives? It is a sad commentary and one I cannot go deeply into here. In contrast I can cite several examples of the opposite.

The most relaxed unions I find are those between two creative people, where both husband and wife are engaged seriously in some phase of artistic endeavor, not necessarily the same. They may be extremely busy—and they often are —but they are relaxed *with each other*. I am thinking of a husband-and-wife team of authors in which the wife writes the text and the husband does the illustrations. The results are some of the most sensitive and beautiful books for children I have ever seen. They have managed this for over thirty years, and through all the vicissitudes of raising a family.

Another couple does almost as well. He writes plays; she writes novels and nonfiction. Each has his own study. More importantly, each is the other's best critic. When the pressures of life (and the more successful one becomes, the greater they are, naturally) force them to "run for their lives," as they put it, they run together. And there is no forwarding address and no telephone.

If a husband is not also an artist, he is sometimes his wife's most loyal supporter and protector. I know of a painter whose husband arranges all her one-woman shows and is the first to greet her guests, beaming with pride. He built an addition to their home in order to give her the north light she needed and is in every way what every woman artist dreams of having for a husband. That he is equally successful as an architect, and that she is just as generous a supporter of his work, must also be mentioned. One could not be true without the other.

One lucky woman writer was presented one Christmas with a small studio which her husband had had built in a far corner of their property so that she might write beyond the reach of telephone and family demands. "Some wives might rather have mink coats," she said, "but I was given what I needed most—solitude for my soul." Another husband lets his poet-wife spend a portion of every day in a room in a neighboring convent, where behind heavy doors is perfect solitude, and only an occasional muffled bell to mar the quiet.

Here we come to a second important consideration: The most fortuitous solution to the problem of how a woman can live out both aspects of her nature, especially as it is manifested in art, is probably through *alternation*. The Hindus knew all about this principle. Their whole society was based on it. A man spent so many years with his family, earning a living, helping to raise children, etc. Then in late middle life he might leave the family circle and seek his spiritual salvation.

I once knew a professor of English who taught for six months only, in spite of strong administrative pressure to go on full time, and then each year retired to a farm with no telephone to write her novels. While on campus she devoted herself exclusively to the business of teaching, and the equally demanding sideline of student-counseling. She said she could never have maintained two careers if she had ever tried to combine them. "Anyway," she said, "the nervous system rebels at monotony. I am a better writer because I do something else part of the time, and I know I'm a much better teacher because I know writing firsthand."

It may be argued that this small minority of women is not worth making such a fuss about. Let the woman artist find her salvation where she can. If the gift is great enough it will find a way. Let her stay in that spinster flat. Who cares if her marriage fails? Let her keep her "hobbies," but who can take them seriously? Women are natively not as "creative" as men. (The hell you say, is our collective response!) And so on, and so on.

Women are as responsible as men for this kind of non-sense. All of us must realize sooner or later that the little girl whose only gifts are creative will grow, if she is permitted,

11

into the kind of woman who has fulfilled all sides of her nature, not just one, and who is thereby capable of adding to the world's treasure, as well as her own. This is the kind of wholeness to which we all aspire—men as well as women. Let man honor this in his wife or his daughter, for only in this wholeness can there be clarity and light between them, and possibly a new and freer relationship.

Part I: As Poet

Chapter 1: Journey Toward Poetry

RECENTLY an acquaintance asked to read a poem of mine just published in a literary magazine. It was forty lines in length. She made appropriate noises of appreciation, then took off her glasses, and asked, as one might inquire about a new recipe for angel food, "Mrs. Burden, *how long* did it take you to write that poem?"

I made a brisk calculation. "About seven months," I replied.

My friend's disbelief, not to say consternation, at such an answer indicates the general lack of awareness on the part of the reading public of what actually goes into the writing of poetry. Not that all poems take seven months. But they are seldom, if ever, as my friend supposed, "poured out of you, sort of divinely inspired."

I am not sure that anything I say here about my own creative process may go far toward illuminating the ignorance of others, but possibly it may help *me* to understand a little more about this mysterious area of human activity. That it *is* mysterious I never doubt, and precisely because of this I keep pecking away at it. Even this revelation will be only a small part of the story, and possibly the least important part. But because even this may be of some interest and value to others—as well as to myself—engaged in this difficult art form, or to readers of poetry, I shall attempt to describe it. The most important part, I repeat, is mystery, and I am sure will remain so, despite science, ESP, or more elaborate computers. In the long run we can probably thank God for that!

The title of this book was borrowed from a poem by May Sarton that originally appeared in *Saturday Review*. I would like to quote just the last stanza because it is about this very experience of writing a poem:

> After the mad beautiful racing is done,
> To be still, to be silent, to stand by a window
> Where time not motion changes light to shadow,
> Is to be present at the birth of creation.
> Now from the falling chaos of sensation
> A single image possesses the whole soul:
> The field of wheat, the telegraph pole.
> From them the composed imagination reaches
> Up and down to find its own frontier.
> All landscapes crystalize and focus here,
> And in the distance stand five copper beeches.

"Journey Toward Poetry," from *The Land of Silence*: Rinehart, New York, 1953: copyright May Sarton. By permission of the author.

If writing a poem is indeed a journey, what kind of

journey is it? I would say it is an interior journey, partly of the bloodstream, partly of the spirit, moving from the unconscious to the conscious, from the unknown to the known, from inspiration to manipulation, from vision to revision. The amateur, the person who is not really a poet but merely has some feeling to let off, goes only part way and thinks he has arrived. It takes not only talent and skill but literary guts to go the whole distance.

In the first place, what kind of person writes poems? What makes John Doe a poet instead of a refrigerator salesman? Or Jane Doe a poet instead of a nurse or a belly dancer? (Some of us, of course, are a little of all three!) Primarily, I think (as Auden said) a poet is one who is fascinated by language as a thing in itself, and he is a person who has not lost the sense of wonder. No matter how sophisticated a poet may be, he must be able to live with his nerve ends exposed, and he must be able at will to lay bare a core that Elizabeth Bowen describes as a "responsive, querying innocence." He must be able to explore his own amazement —to quote Christopher Fry. He must be a person on whom nothing is lost—Henry James. He must be the kind of person who can look at cracks in a floor or the tracings of a wave on a piece of driftwood and see something the casual passerby does not see. He must be able to invest the ordinary episodes of daily life with the unordinary raiment of his imagination.

One of the disciplines a poet learns early in life is to keep his attention *en garde*. Not only is he by nature curious, but he is interested in all kinds of relationships and, particularly, in the eccentric relationship we call *paradox*: how the small is really the universe; how the moving seems to stand still (Frances Minturn Howard has a lovely example of this— among many—in her poem about a snowstorm in Boston, and it was the snow that was motionless while the buildings seemed to fall down); how illusion is often truth, etc. For this he needs not only an observant eye but the intelligence and wit to translate what he sees into words. Poetry is not written by sentimental old ladies (or young ones), oozing self-expression, but by sensitively alive, clearheaded, technically skilled craftsmen who write poems because it is their way of experiencing life. And it is the hardest work in the world.

Yeats once said, "It is not inspiration that exhausts one, it is art." And art begins with a rumbling in the mind. But not *any* mind. For me, the kind of mental state that is most apt to produce a poem is similar to what a psychic cultivates for her experiments in clairvoyance: a relaxed alertness. For this the upper cerebral processes have to be slightly unhinged from the lower. (That, cries my nonpoetic friend, who is sure all poets are a little crazy, explains everything!) A kind of casual dissociation is ideal—like doing something with your hands and letting the mind fly free. I find that ironing is ideal; so is scrubbing the kitchen floor, but more wearing. Other occupations are also salutary—listening to music (especially Mozart); driving a car (Hildegarde Flanner always takes pad and pencil with her on long drives alone and jots down ideas, probably at risk to life and limb); traveling. (For some reason most people find that planes are less conducive to creativity than trains or boats. Perhaps there is too much tension on planes, too many people in too small an area.)

One thing is certain—one will never write a poem by determining to do so. One must learn how to catch a poem off guard. In this connection, I recall an example used once by Alan Watts to illustrate some metaphysical truth of Zen. It is just as applicable to poetry. He said that the only way to see those fascinating little "sky flowers" that drift before your vision in sunlight is to look somewhere else and catch one out of the corner of your eye. You will never see one if you stare straight at it. This also applies to magical visions of all sorts and to enchanting creatures such as elves and goblins. They're always seen just disappearing around the edge of a flowerpot. But, as Mr. Watts was fond of pointing out, all sorts of very important things in the world must only be looked at out of the corner of one's eye.

And so it is with the beginnings of a poem. For if one does

not stalk a poem with rifle and hound, one will occasionally bump smack into one. The object may be something actually sensed—a child standing alone on the steps of a cathedral, a handful of dried grasses in a blue vase, the screaming of a bird in a cat's claw—but it will be seen as though lit up with inner neon. Or it may be something much vaguer—an itch of irritation, a swell of anguish, a nudging of insight—that suddenly breaks into words.

This is the *donnée*—the given—and there is seldom any doubt about it. It seems to come bearing a flag. One seizes it with a glad cry of recognition. Once I was given such a line in the middle of a busy intersection in Chicago, and I could hardly make it to the other side of the street I was so excited. (Oddly enough, I am more often given the last line of a poem than the first.) On another occasion I dreamed a line and on waking wrote it down. That line still waits for its poem. I told this story to my Poetry Workshop one night, and a member returned the next week with her development of my *donnée*. Not bad, either.

Sometimes these *donnée* are merely phrases; sometimes they are whole lines. The only way I know how to anchor them is to scribble them on scraps of paper and stuff them into a folder. My life is unfortunately too busy to work on them often or for long. Every so often I read through this folder—always bulging—to see what still interests me. It is amazing stuff—most of it seems to have been written by someone I never met. In the majority of instances *I have no recollection either of thinking such things or of having written them down.*

Another way of putting it might be that one plants a lot of seeds and then makes periodic examinations to see which of them, if any, have sprouted. Sometimes it is the least likely.

It is at this point in the process that the artisan side of the poet asserts itself, and the hardheaded critic works side by side with the always uncritical, childlike artist. From now on the intellect has to shape, form, slap, and knead the raw material into something structured—into a poem. Feeling doesn't stop and thinking begin. It is far less simple than that. But they work together, with cerebrum always having the last word.

Karl Shapiro once observed that genius in poetry was only the intuitive knowledge of form, and I am inclined to agree with him. A textbook on forms can give a poet all he is supposed to know of rhythm, meter, and language, but there is nothing to tell him which words to choose and how to let them fall in the line except his own sense of what is right. That sense he has built up unconsciously through his own life experience, not just through the reading of other poems or through his previous trials and errors in writing, helpful though these are. One is told that one must have a good ear—whatever that really is—and I know it is true, but I do not know how one develops such an ear, or what to do if one does not have it. Whenever a student asks me how to tell which form is right for a poem and which is wrong, I stammer some nonsense about how it *feels* right, or *sounds* right, and I am reminded of the Whitney Darrow cartoon of the two moppets in ballet school, one of whom is saying smugly to the other, "You've either got it or you haven't got it."

One thing I am sure of is that every poem brings its own form, its own architecture, much as the seed brings its own plant. One cannot build a poem the way one builds a house. It is partly an organic process—an interrelation between what one is given and what one makes of the given—of insight and artifice. A poem not only grows under intellect and imagination, it also seems to grow from the inside out. One follows as best one can the thrusts into air of one's seedling. When an editor once said that he liked my poems because they were not concocted but secreted, he was stating a half-truth. (Why are half-truths sometimes so much more brilliant-sounding than whole truths?) A successful poem is *both* secreted and concocted, and it is difficult, if not impossible, to tell just where one ends and the other begins.

Two subjects need further word. One is cadence, or

rhythm. If one writes free verse, as I do, the problem of cadence is important. Sometimes it seems to present itself with the first scrap of paper. It is elusive, seemingly accidental, and, again, intuitive. Whenever it is found it seems to approximate the speaking voice of the poet. Which is why, I suppose, one can recognize in any collection of a poet's work a *style*, a consistency of auditory impression, regardless of other factors. People have said they would know a poem of mine anywhere even if it were unsigned. This could be that I have mannerisms (and I'm sure I do), or it could mean that I have found my own voice. (Or possibly, both.) The latter is a virtue, the former a vice.

Another whole field of inquiry, intimately related to style, is *imagery*. What concrete images one chooses (and a poet had better translate his abstractions into them if he is going to hope to write a successful poem) depend on everything the poet has read, felt, experienced, as well as on his genes, his temperament, his blood pressure, and his glands. I am sure if one were wise enough, one could psychoanalyze a personality solely on the basis of the imagery he uses in his collected poems. For example, John Holmes told me how his class once classified the images of a well-known poet, and discovered he seldom if ever used a word denoting color. When the poet was told of this he was upset. This seemed to him a disreputable lack in his own personality, though I am sure an analyst would merely find that he was a person with weak visual images, but was perhaps more moved by auditory images. I, myself, seldom use color words and am overly fascinated by *stones*, *bones*, and *trees*, and indefinite images like *air*, *sun*, *grass*, *sky*, *rose*. These belong to the constant environment I carry about with me and against which I relate whatever event or experience has set off the poem. In other words, whatever I have stored over the years in the remote quadrants of my being nourish and determine what language I will ultimately choose, consciously and unconsciously, for the experience I am trying to re-create. And this is true, of course, of all poets.

In actual practice, this is rather a disorderly business—on

the surface, at least. The original piece of paper on which is scribbled my first idea or line has collected over an interval of days, weeks, or even months, a series of such scraps, all sizes and shapes, held together with a paper clip. The paper clip may have given way to a rubber band, or the whole mess stuffed into an envelope. This *clustering* of other ideas, lines, images is a sign that sprouting is taking place. Something is growing, and at its own speed. A sense of urgency is building up. (If it doesn't, no poem will result.) I try to force the growth a little. After all, it was last spring that I first had that wonderful inspiration. I begin to fidget. My unconscious promptly clams up and refuses to tell me a thing. I am hopelessly stuck. I nag at it a little more. Nothing happens. I decide to pay no attention to it, and go outside to rake leaves. Suddenly the tension inside me becomes unbearable. I rush indoors, grab a fresh sheet of paper, and begin to write. Everything else is forgotten until out of this disorder some order, some shape, emerges. There is a sigh of relief when the first good draft appears. Then more tedium while it is polished and honed. A word won't come right. I let it alone and prepare dinner. In the middle of the night the right word is there hanging in the air above my bed. I grab it and write it down. The next day another fresh paper, and the tenth revision. Finally it is ready to show one trusted friend. A week later, with cooler eyes, I review it again. Something is not quite right in the fourth line—there, that's better. So it goes with most poems. To be specific, let me take the poem originally in question—forty lines, seven months.

LANDSCAPE FOR STONES

For E.B. of Big Sur

Like children in search of surprise
we crept through the pinching gate,
leaving the meadow behind,
leaving sheep, tame to our eyes,
and small birds in the grass.

You wore your red hat;
I carried poems. You took my hand
and pointed upward. We saw the cormorants pass.

Then the dunes broke open
and we fell from time,
upon sand
unmarked except by tide,
upon water filling half the world,
and flung against a sky as wide.

(We were not children then;
we were not even young.)

We entered softly, pretending no fear.
You walked from me along the soapy edges of the surf;
I scooped a hollow from immensity,
and made a pillow of your shoes.

But there was no welcome here.
We were a bruise
upon the land.

This was country not for men—
for stones, perhaps, or fish that never learned to climb.
It was a landscape poets dread.
Our symbols freeze: the sea is sea;
the bird a nameless bird.
We are not gods to leave our trace
on rock or air.
We belong to seasons
and to time.

I would have told you this
but you were half a mile away,
measuring your small height against the sky,
metaphor, mortal,
precious to my eye,
and loudly in this empty, wordless place
(though you could not have heard)
I called against the wind
one fierce, defiant word.

From *Naked as the Glass* by Jean Burden: October House, New York, 1963.

I started with a most mundane, prosaic object—a pair of shoes. The experience involved an afternoon on a strange deserted beach at Big Sur with poet Eric Barker. It was my first visit, and it had all the elements of which poems are made—a setting, a person, natural aspects that could also be symbols. All these were evidently stirring about in my mind when I tore a page out of a notebook and wrote down the next day some of the lines that were "given." "And made a pillow of your shoes" was the first. "In this nonverbal world / give me one word" was also scrawled on that first scrap. This last does not survive just this way, but the idea does. Also the idea of the separation between Eric and me on the beach, the observing of the figure against the sky. But the mood is quite different in the beginning from what eventually comes through.

Nothing happens with these fragments for some months. I finally attempt to write something down in stanza form; I am searching not only for a first line, but for the cadence, the right rhythm and shape for the poem. The result is prosy, but I have some movement in the first verse—and one good line: "We had left the meadow behind, and the pinching gate." I recall that "pinching gate" was one of those happy phrases that also seemed "given." I am beginning to explore the idea of *time* (it is one of my major preoccupations), but in the second verse, except for "You walked along the soapy edges of the surf," I have gone off into a bypath which probably will be another poem someday—"This extended 'I,' what was its shape? I, with my father's mouth and my mother's eyes, named for a Scotch girl I never knew. . . ." Whoa! I'm off the track. This digression I discard, but there is a germ there of an entirely new poem. I won't throw it away.

On the margin of this first attempt I have written in pencil a note: "This is no water to swim in, only to look upon, not too close, *where all abstraction is distilled to rock and sea and one frail man.*" This idea is developed in later versions and, in fact, becomes a dominant theme.

More months go by. The fragment lies in the folder

untouched. Every once in a while I take it out and look at it, wince at its clumsiness, put it away again. But all the while it is cooking gently on the back burner of my mind. In the small interstices of my busy days—a daily job, commuting, cooking, cleaning, editing, writing prose, etc.—it is slowly coming to a boil.

One day I catch hold of a first line as it is flying past my nose (metaphors change rapidly in this discussion) and quickly I write it down on a handy piece of yellow paper. It brought with it some lines of its own:

> *Like children in search of a kingdom* (this is going to have
>   one change later)
> *we had crept through the pinching gate*
> *leaving the meadow behind*
> *and the sheep*
> *and come suddenly upon this place*
> *as though for the first time.*

But wham! I am stuck again. The second stanza goes back to the original playing with the concept of time. I put it all together with a paper clip and go back to my dusting. My mind is playing with other metaphysical ideas—all of them affirmative. Later all of these change.

Subsequent scraps of paper take Eric and me only a little further: "the dunes opened / and we came suddenly upon this place / as lonely and sharp as a gull's cry." One little piece has on it "leaving the meadow / and small birds in the grass." I am beginning to find contrast in what we leave behind—a good idea which I later develop more fully. On the same bit is the first indication that this poem contains emotions of dread and terror—something I had not expected in the beginning. Did I actually experience terror subconsciously? Probably. Or am I now imagining it? This is how experience becomes transmuted in the writing of it. This is how we discover ourselves.

The next page contains a new line, almost prose. It is the first playing around with the idea I noted earlier about *abstraction being distilled*. I have written:

This was the world all poets know in dream
the land of favorite symbols—but now the metaphor is real

I don't know what I really think about this, so I let it alone for a while.

A week or so later I take another good look. I am not pleased. Something is very wrong with this poem. What is the matter with it? The opposite of what is usually the matter with a first draft: it is too compact, too compressed for the ideas I seem to be trying to express. It needs letting out, like a dress that is too small. The hem must be let down; a gusset here and a gusset there; perhaps a whole new top. And I must move from abstractions to specifics. There isn't enough visual imagery; not enough concrete details. But I do have the right cadence, though I have not yet found a way to use rhyme, and somehow I feel acutely the need of it.

I keep my first line, but with one important change— "Like children in search of *surprise*"—this gets away from a near cliché, and I found it in the simple process of looking for something to rhyme with "eyes." The mood of loneliness is now well established, the hostility between man and nature, but I haven't given up the idea that in the last few lines I am going to show affirmation, a victory of man over nature.

I won't note all the subsequent drafts, revisions, crossings-out that follow over a period of weeks of agonizing effort. I am in quiet torment. It will not let me alone. I carry the folder back and forth to work. It lies on the seat of the car beside me. In heavy traffic I steal a look at it. I find I can use rhyme to link the stanzas together. I break up stanzas, put them together again. I throw away lumps of ideas. I linger over words, polishing, taking up, and putting down. All the way through I am bothered by tenses. Eleven sheets of paper lie one on top of the other from this point to the final version. Eleven attempts to make it say what I want to say. Eleven hellish efforts to be true to the poem. I have to type out each revision. Seeing the whole poem on paper helps enormously to see where the faults still lie. Reading it aloud also helps.

Several times I think I have it finished. For an hour or so I am in ecstasy. Then I read it again. No, something is still wrong. I take another piece of paper.

My main problem finally narrows down to the last stanza. I have myself fleeing the beach, looking back at the small figure of Eric against the sky, and I still have the idea that man is triumphant against this wild landscape. My last line in fact uses the very word "triumphant." I can't see that I am saying too much.

At this point I need an audience. I telephone a critical friend and read her the poem. She is silent at the end. Then she says, "It is wonderful—except for the ending. I thought I understood exactly what you were saying until I heard the last line. Now I'm not at all sure."

I take another fresh look. Of course. I understand. I have to back up to a *penultimate* point in my insight. My actual vision *was* triumphant, but for the sake of the poem, for the sake of artistic wholeness, I must be *partial* in insight. How ironic. The ultimate vision of the triumph of man over landscape, or of the harmony between man and apparently hostile nature, between opposites—this must wait for a sequel. I am trying to say too much. I must move back to what, metaphysically, is an imperfect or, rather, inconclusive concept.

> And loudly in this empty, wordless place
> (though you could not have heard)
> I called against the wind
> one fierce, defiant word.

I keep the terror, and the poem is saved by this poetic duplicity.

Was it Valéry who said something about how a true poem is never finished, only abandoned? But before we abandon it we must have determined exactly at what point in space and time to set *five copper beeches* (to quote May Sarton again). Perhaps it is a futile pastime to try to describe how one writes a poem, for the stuff of poetry itself is as elusive as quicksilver. This was the metaphor Hildegarde

Flanner used in the introduction to an anthology of college verse, and it serves me well here: ". . . it is a captive and restless treasure to hold. It is heavy for its slight and shining volume. It is solid yet it flows. It is distilled yet it lives. It is a mineral with a mind. It is eternal matter. . . . It is the stuff of our sober astonishment, the concentration of itself without hindrance, and if it is not spilled, it is poetry."*

*From "Foreword" to Sweet Briar Anthology, published by Sweet Briar College, Sweet Briar, Virginia, May 1956.

Chapter 2: *Another Poem and How It Grew*

I DON'T KNOW how long it took me to write "Invisible Tree," nor do I consider it more than a mildly interesting statistic how long it took anyone to do anything. I do know that it gave me a very bad time.

The first stirrings antedated by months any notation on paper. I remember brooding about the Adam and Eve legend and thinking that the accepted version of their being driven out of the garden because of the sin of the apple didn't

27

satisfy me. From my own unorthodox point of view they had to leave to find a context in which they could develop as human beings. Staying in that lush Paradise with fruit dripping off the trees would be to stay forever in innocence. Growth was only possible *outside*.   SEE FIGURE I

Reproduced here is my first scrap of paper, headed (as they always are headed) simply "*Poem*." It was begun one day at breakfast where a pad of paper and pencil are always handy. Underlined are the lines and phrases that survive. There are only two that remain intact, but others endure in idea. As so often happens with me, I was given the last line first: "We had never meant to stay." Except for the change of pronoun, this lasts through all the tortuous backings and fillings that lie ahead. There is also the phrase "gentles the exile," which I keep.

I have the beginnings of a first line: "For this the garden closes." There are other things, mostly prosy, but evocative for the future: "It was right that we choose what we did"; "It was not the world but the world's womb"; "the sun at their backs" (see what happens to this in later versions); and "it was a long time before they understood why they had to go." I am putting down tentative ideas. That they did not always fall into poetry was not at this time important. Some did and some did not. But if I did not put my thumb on these elusive wisps of thought as they floated by, I would lose them forever. How many times a haunting phrase will occur to me as I am driving a car. I think I will surely remember it until I get to a paper and pencil, only to have it fade or twist before I can snare it.   SEE FIGURE 2

The second working paper carries me only a little further. "Green / gray" heads the small sheet; then "conceive not only their children but the world." This fragment develops into a good deal. Then comes "silken grass" and "rim of wilderness," with "hem" as an alternative for "rim." Obviously this poem is going to be longer than some. I have too much to say, and much of it is under the layer of consciousness I call my mind. Digging it out is not going to be easy. This is actually the first time I have ever thought deeply

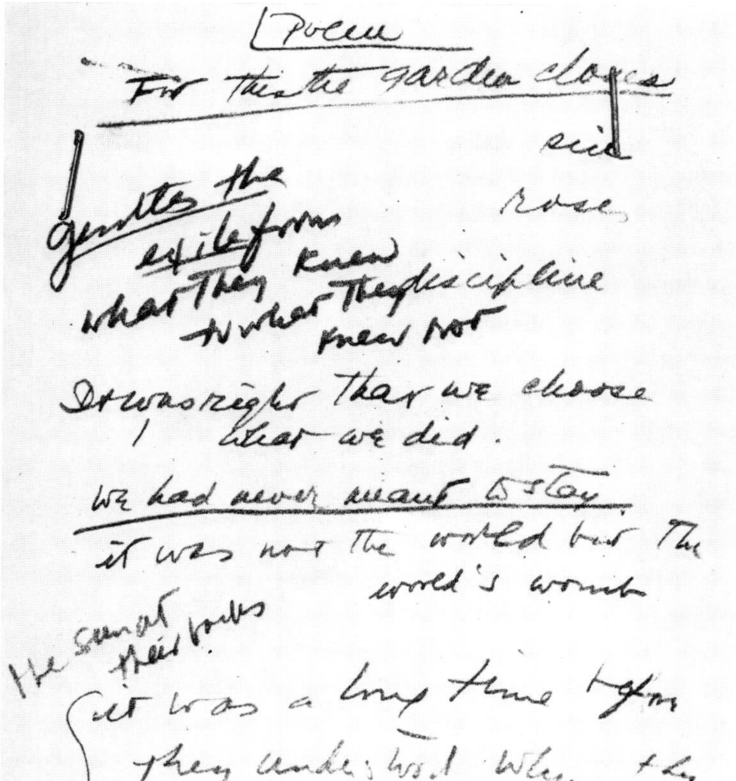

Figure 1

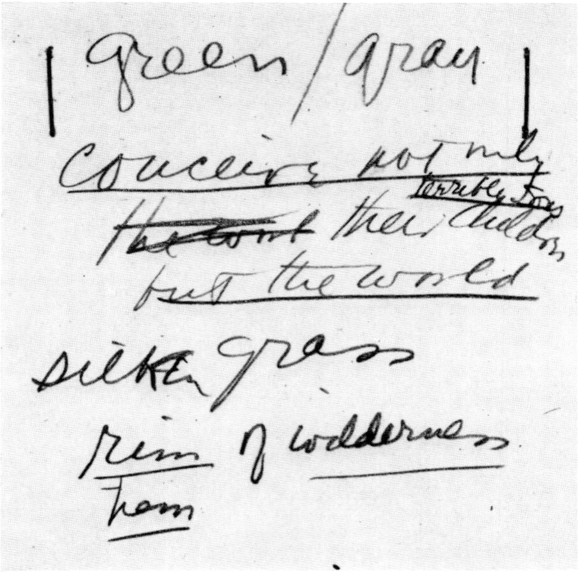

Figure 2

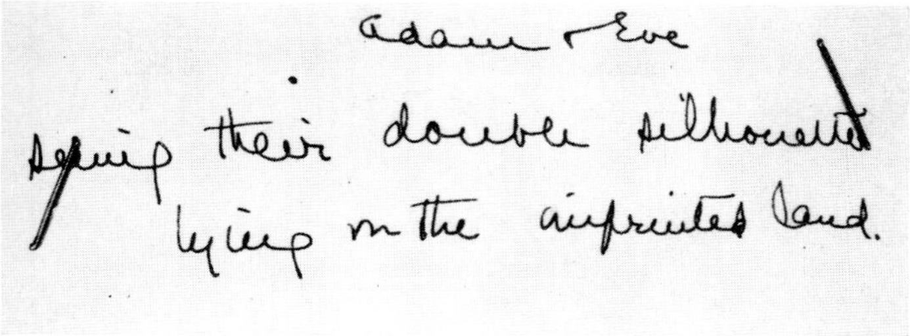

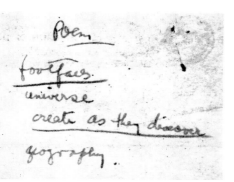

Adam & Eve

leaving their double silhouette
lying on the unprinted sand.

Figure 3

Poem

footfalls
universe
create as they discover
geography.

Figure 4

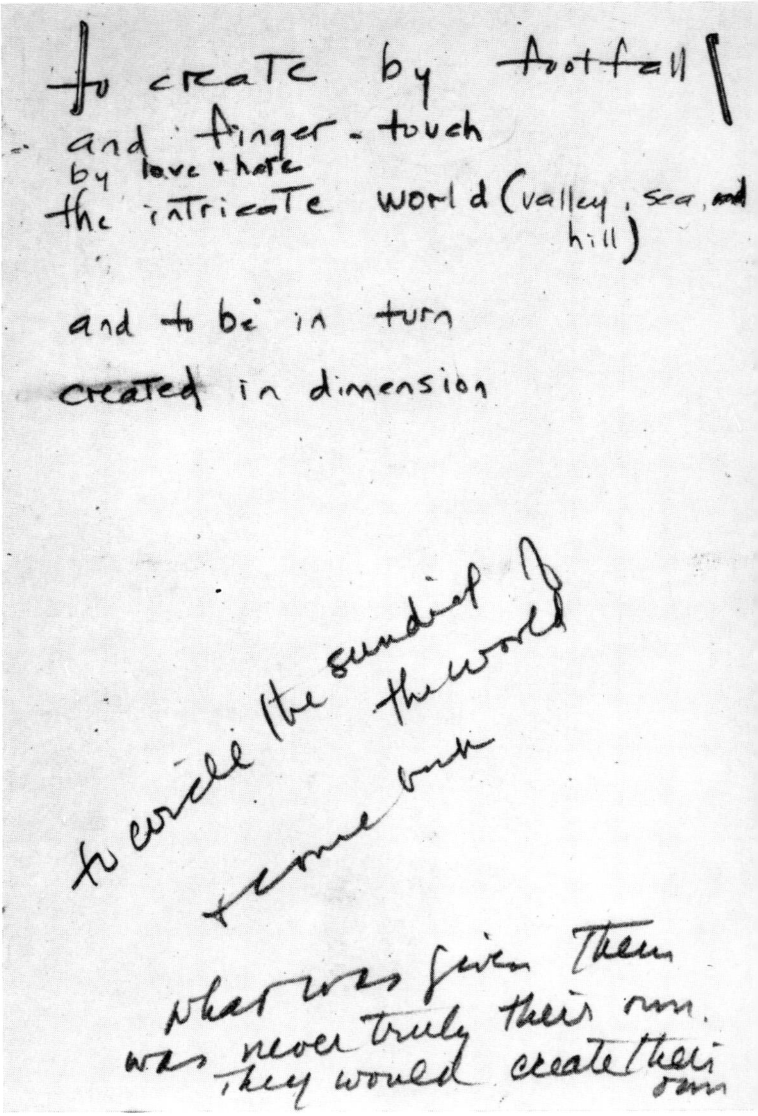

to create by footfall
and finger-touch
by love & hate
the intricate world (valley, sea, and
                              hill)

and to be in turn

created in dimension

to circle (the sundial
                    the world
                        come back

what was given them
was never truly their own.
they would create their
                        own

Figure 5

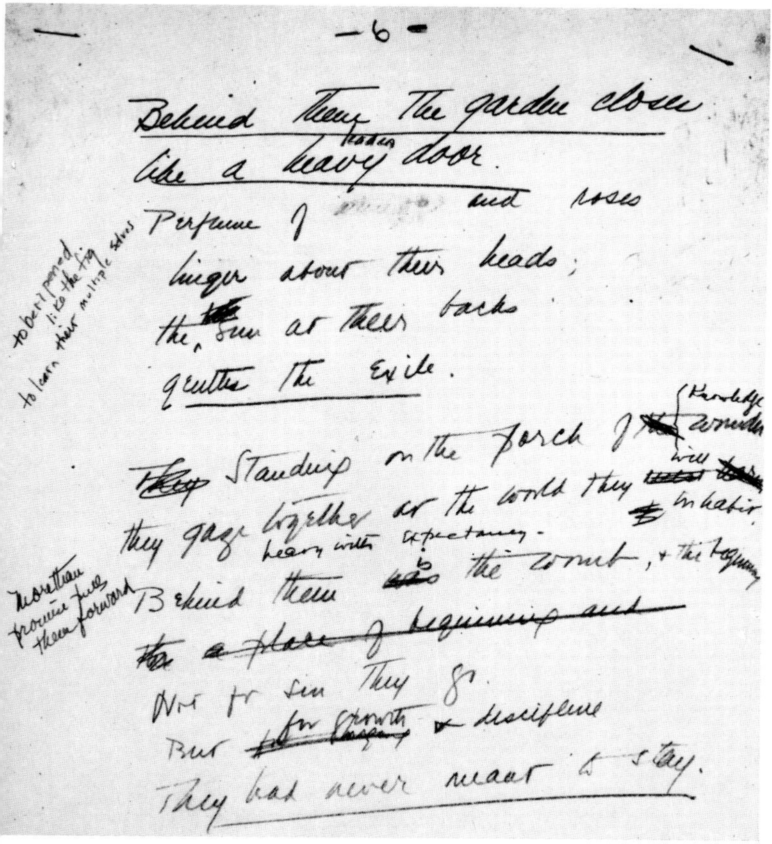

Behind <del>them</del> The garden closes
like a <del>heavy</del> door.

Perfume of <del>xxxx</del> and roses
linger about their heads;
the <del>xxx</del> sun at their backs
gentles the Exile.

<del>They</del> Standing on the porch of <del>xxxx</del>
they gaze together at the world they <del>will</del> <del>xxx</del> inhabit
Behind them <del>lies</del> the womb, + the beginning
<del>the a place</del> <del>of beginning and</del>
Not for sin They go.
But <del>for leaving</del> for growth & discipline
They had never meant to stay.

to be inspired
life the fig serve
to learn their multiple skins

more than
promise pulls
them forward

(Knowledge
wonder

Figure 6

The porch of wonder!
look toward the imperfect season plain &
where they must learn to live
the mangoes & figs behind them, ripe on the
valley floor.

Figure 7

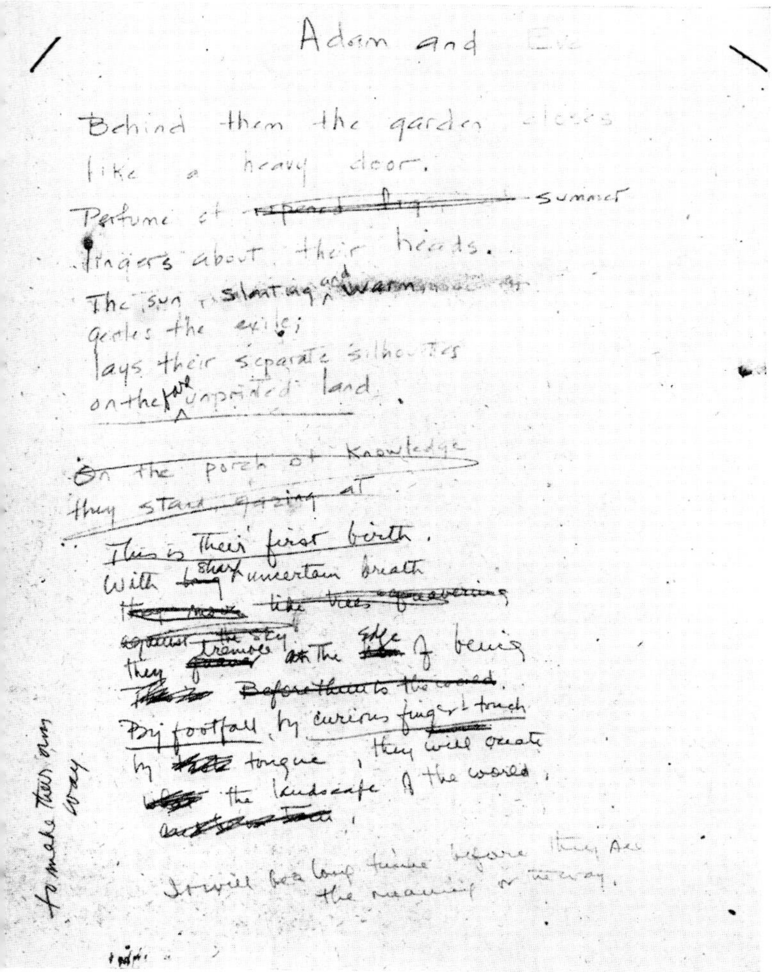

Adam and Eve

Behind them the garden closes
like a heavy door.
Perfume of ~~sweet fig~~ summer
lingers about their heads.
The sun ~~slanting~~ and warm
gentles the exiles
lays their separate silhouettes
on the ~~pale~~ unprinted land.

~~On the porch of Knowledge~~
~~they stare gazing at~~
    This is their first birth.
With ~~long~~ sharp uncertain breath
~~they move like trees quavering~~
~~against the sky~~ they ~~tremble~~ at the ~~edge~~ of being
~~This is~~ ~~Before them to the world~~
By footfall, by curious finger touch
by ~~their~~ tongue, they will create
~~this~~ the landscape of the world.
~~and~~ ~~then~~

    It will be a long time before they ~~know~~
        the meaning or the way.

To make their own way (margin note)

Figure 8

about the Adam and Eve myth, and I do not understand all I
know about it! SEE FIGURE 3

A third scrap is entitled "Adam and Eve." It is a working
title only. I am quite sure I will finally give it something less
obvious, though titles are not my strong point. I am beginning to realize I need more visual imagery, and I have
scrawled in almost illegible handwriting "seeing their
double silhouettes lying on the unprinted land" (cf. final
version).

On the back of a receipt for my driver's license I find
random jottings: SEE FIGURE 4

POEM

footfall
universe
create as they discover
geography

It is not until sheet No. 5 that I make any real progress and
it is still without an opening line. Consequently I don't yet
have the poem's cadence. Instead I am bumping around in
the semidark, looking for it. SEE FIGURE 5

to create by footfall
and finger-touch
the intricate world (valley, sea, and hill)
and to be in turn
created in dimension

In the middle is written "to circle the sundial of the world
and come back", and at the bottom, squished up in the
corner, are the words: "what was given them was never
truly their own. They would create their own."

So far, mostly prose. I fidget and fret through days of
daily, nonpoetic living.

Sheet No. 6: Well, at last, a first line, and the right movement: SEE FIGURE 6

Behind them the garden closes
like a heavy door.

Now I feel I am on my way. It is a breakthrough. Without
hesitation I follow with:

29

Perfume of   and roses
linger about their heads;
the sun at their backs
gentles the exile.

Standing on the porch of knowledge
they gaze together at the world they will inhabit
heavy with expectancy
Behind them is the womb and the beginning.
Not for sin they go,
but for growth and discipline.

They had never meant to stay.

The first stanza needs work, but it is on the right track. The rest of it, except for the last line, is terrible. Heavy with abstractions and ploddings, it is as pedestrian as a tired donkey. Never mind, I have the first line and the last, and that means direction. All I need is a middle.

On a page largely confined to a large doodle of a cat are some scribblings: SEE FIGURE 7

the porch of wonder

(I like this, evidently, but can't use it.)

look toward the imperfect plain
     where they must learn to live
the mangoes and figs behind them, ripe on the valley
     floor

If you ask me, I never should have attempted a subject as done-to-death and metaphysically complicated as Adam and Eve. Maybe Karl Shapiro has said it all anyway.

I take time to go shopping. Days pass. Adam and Eve are right where I left them, and nothing has moved at all. Then one evening as I am listening to 'The Trout Quintet', I get another line: "This is their first birth." It seems to be good. I go back to my first line and start again.   SEE FIGURE 8

Behind them the garden closes
like a heavy door.

Perfume of summer
lingers about their heads.
The sun, slanting and warm,
gentles the exile;

lays their separate silhouettes
on the bare unprinted land.

This is their first birth.
With sharp uncertain breath
they move like trees quavering*
against the sky,*
they tremble at the edge of being.

By footfall, by curious finger-touch,
by tongue, they will create
the landscape of the world.

It will be a long time before they see
the meaning or the way.

*These two lines are crossed out.

I am well on my way to rounding out the picture of the two lonely people at the threshold of the world. The garden is behind them, but that is not tragedy, I insist. It is the *world* that is out there. And, as I know I say over and over, *the world is good.* (It is true, I suppose, that every poem is unwittingly a metaphysical statement.)

The rest is relatively easy. I know where I am going. Yet even as I write that, I realize it is *not* easy except as one has learned it through the pain of rejecting over and over within oneself the half-baked, facile, false leads that produce only imitations of poetry. It is a harsh lifetime struggle and it never really ends. But once the choice is made—and it had better be made early in one's career—it is never undone. From then on, nothing less than the best one can do is ever permitted to stand.

Specifically, this means for "Adam and Eve" (and for many poems) a sharpening of verbs and nouns and a winnowing of all but the essential adverbs and adjectives. This means, of course, a sharper focusing of one's vision. One is closing in on one's subject. In the fourth line, for instance, I change "lingers about" to "halos." The philosophic insights begin to find their right visual imagery. "With sharp, quivering breath / they taste the new air. / For better or ill / what lies before them / is their kingdom. / With a look they draw it toward them." The two statements: "This is their first birth" and "This is the beginning of the world," I set off by single lines. Punctuation is another device for making the poem say what you want it to say—a simple device, but often one of the most effective.

The previous three lines that tried to tell of Adam and Eve's act of creation were obviously too brief. I expand them, and in so doing employ a list of images, some definite, some more indefinite: "With footfall and finger-touch / they will create in time / moss, pear, bird, and violet, / river, field, valley, hill."

What is the difference in function between the definite and indefinite image? I am not entirely sure, but I think one instinctively reaches for the indefinite (or, more precisely, *less* definite) image ("bird," "river," "field," "valley", "hill") when one is using it to carry on its back the freight of philosophic concepts. The more definite the image, the more personal and, therefore, more emotional the effect. Though this is certainly a philosophic poem, I tried to vary the imagery in this respect. "Flower" would have been less definite than "violet," so in this category I chose the latter. "Fruit" would have been less definite than "pear." By jumbling definite and indefinite together, I implied, I hope, both the personal and the universal.

In the next versions I notice too a working-over of lines for the value of *sound*. The line "but to make forever visible" was scratched out and "but to unshadow" written above. This kind of thing is what every poet does with almost every poem, and those amateurs who think that revising and polishing are only for the inexpert are not only wrong but 180 degrees wrong.

The idea of "the invisible tree / in the Eden of the mind" was another *donnée*—the kind that often comes as one digs deeper into one's own mind for the last drop of meaning, the last flicker of vision. Without it the poem fuzzes, lacks ideational climax. With it, the tension reaches a peak, then relaxes into the conclusion of the last two lines. (I also picked up the final title, but that of course was incidental.) Here is the final version.

32

INVISIBLE TREE

Behind them the garden closes
like a heavy door.
Perfume of summer
halos their heads.
The sun, slanting and warm,
gentles the exile;
lays their silhouettes
on the bare, unprinted land.

This is their first birth.

With sharp, quivering breath
they taste the new air.
For better or ill
what lies before them
is their kingdom.
With a look they draw it toward them.

This is the beginning of the world.

With footfall and finger-touch
they will create in time
moss, pear, bird, and violet,
river, field, valley, hill.

Alone, with hands like wands,
they too are gods.

It is for this they broke the circle—
not just to bear their sons,
but to unshadow with their blazing eyes
the invisible tree
in the Eden of the mind.

Later, when they no longer weep,
they too will know
they had never meant to stay.

From *Naked as the Glass* by Jean Burden: October House, New York, 1963.

Something should be said here for the dramatic quality of poetry. I am a firm believer that poems should have a beginning, a middle, and an end; that they should build to a climax, and resolve. Sometimes (often, in fact) my climax is in the last line, and the resolving goes on in the reader's mind. But I don't think I have ever written a poem totally without dramatic tension. Something has to *happen* in a poem. It must take you from *here* to *there*. I am impatient with poems that peter out at the end. I want to be left with that mixture of pain and delight that accompanies a slight electric shock. Then I know that for me the poem has succeeded.

It was a great surprise to me, therefore, to have a critic say that I wrote poems that stood still. As far as I am concerned, nothing could be further from the truth. It is true that they are without violence, that they are, on the surface, quiet. But they are in no sense *slack*. Action is going on at a much deeper level than kinesthetic, as other critics observed. ("Leashed intensity" was one of the phrases used.) To have this quality at all, one must have energy. Not physical energy, necessarily—no one has less than I—but emotional energy. One must constantly give oneself away to life in its totality, not merely make judgments about it. And one must have exquisite control. A fountain overflows; a cistern contains. A poem does both.

Behind every poem must be felt the abyss. Depth below depth. What keeps the reader from falling is a thin, taut, protecting wire. Without the abyss *and* the wire there is no poetry that matters.

Chapter 3: My Book is Published

Contrasts in poetry publishing in the last twenty-five years

POETS WHO STUDY the writers' guides on how to get their books of poems into print are not likely to find out. Nor will they learn the trick by asking their friends. Nor will these words of mine, presumably, be any more helpful. They may, however, encourage those who have given up after the first few discouraging letters of rejection—or, at the least, amuse the clan.

I know of one poet whose manuscript was accepted by the first publisher to whom she sent it. I know of one other who was asked by a publisher to allow his firm to publish his work. Most of the rest, like me, went the long, bumpy route.

There is no pain in telling the story today. My book, *Naked as the Glass*, is already in its second printing after a generous first run of 1,500 copies. An amusing letter enclosing a royalty check from David Way of October House (formerly Clarke & Way) begins: "I am furious with you. In the first place I owe you money . . . and in the second place I have to reprint your book. By all odds you should have lasted two years, and at this rate you're never going to make it. Now with this review in *Poetry* you'll probably sell *more* books. . . . A few more books like yours and I won't be able to show a nice comfortable loss in the publishing division."

It would have been nice if at some time during the preceding twelve years I had been granted a prescient glimpse of this letter. It would have made less bleak the preceding decade-plus of writing and waiting, waiting and writing. But no such clairvoyance was granted me. Instead I had to learn to go with it, to bide my time without rancor, to know that when the time was right the book would be born. I am exceedingly impatient by nature. But in this instance the patience I needed I was given. It went hand in hand with my unshaken faith in the book itself. No matter how many times it came back from a publisher in those years, I never really doubted that it would someday be accepted.

This kind of feeling is a knowing-in-the-blood. I do not know how one attains it. It seems to be a grace. If I had not had this certainty I might not have sustained that long interval of failure with as much equanimity as I did. With it, I walked a sure, if perilous, tightrope between absolute pride and absolute humility—and reached the other side.

But all this is hindsight.

In 1950 at the instigation of a friend, Louis Freedman, a well-known publishers' representative, I sent my manuscript to Random House with a personal recommendation from Louis to his old friend Saxe Commins. Nothing could have appeared more propitious, inasmuch as Louis has always judged my work with unqualified enthusiasm, and his accompanying letter should have moved publishers' mountains even in the unhalcyon days of the postwar era. I think I can say without argument that this kind of endorsement, while very pleasant, is ultimately irrelevant. I am sure it made possible, in this instance, a personal perusal by Mr. Commins, rather than by an anonymous reader in the last office down the hall, but I do not think it changed his mind one whit. Nor would it ever influence to any degree the judgment of a publisher who must decide to the best of his ability where his dollars are to be spent. As Mr. Commins wrote: "I wish it were possible to offer you some encouragement as to the possibilities of publishing your work in book form. Unfortunately, the demand for poetry is so slight that we find it difficult even to find a market for the works of our established poets. This is no solace to you, especially since your verses really have lyrical merit, and were it not for these commercial considerations would be worthy of publication."

I see by my file that it was February of 1952 before I tried again. During that interim I wrote more poems, weeded out others, was published in a few good magazines like *Poetry*, *Beloit Poetry Journal*, *Saturday Review*, *Tomorrow*, won a handful of critical posies en route, and had the joy of seeing two of my poems accepted for Borestone Mountain Poetry Awards, anthologies for best poems of the year. Since that time I have had many other poems anthologized in these annual volumes, and elsewhere, but there is nothing to equal the first such notification. In memory it rivals the ecstasy of my first letter of acceptance from *Poetry*. I floated above the earth in a pink haze for a good week, bearing the gentle teasing of my father without a tremor. I remember he called me "Amy Lowell" at every opportunity. I don't know where he found that analogy in his unliterary frame of reference, but it amused him. It tickled me even more when I thought of the dissimilarity between my skinny, long-legged frame and Amy's bulk. The literary discrepancies

were even funnier, I realize now, but I thought very little of
that. In those days of youthful overconfidence it never
occurred to me I couldn't publish a book to rival Amy's any
time I wanted to.

Looking back at the letters that accompanied the return
of my manuscript through 1954—eight submissions, all to
major New York publishers, the first goal of every un-
published writer and of course the hardest to make—certain
themes are repeated over and over: "I'm sure that you
realize how difficult poetry is to market and that publishers
seem to know the sort of thing they can best market. . . .
Despite the obvious quality of your poems, reflecting a
genuine poetic gift, our decision is not to undertake publication."

Ditto from another well-known house: "As you probably know, the present market for poetry is an extremely
poor one. As a result we have not been able to add any poetry
to our list, and have even had difficulty publishing that which
is already under contract. This is a deplorable situation, and
we can only hope that the future will change it and change it
soon."

Another editor wrote: "I have kept your poems so long
because I truly enjoyed them and felt sympathetic to them.
But the facts are that we are crowded with poetry mms., are
trying to hold them down to very few volumes a year, and
are already scheduled into the very end of 1954 or 1955. . . ."

"We have found much to admire in these pages," apolo-
gized another, "and I wish I could be writing you more
inspiringly on the practical side. We cannot publish more
than one or two books of poetry a year, and our advance
commitments are already adequate."

"We think it is a most distinguished collection, but we
have not been publishing poetry in the last few years, and
our final decision was against reversing that policy," wrote
still another New York firm.

With time and effort I could make the book better. But
what could I do about the *Zeitgeist?*

Georgie Starbuck Galbraith put it perfectly:

These are times, believe me, Bards,
When a publisher regards
Poets as a fiscal bane.
Cookbooks sell; so does Spillane;
Even tomes on building muscles.
But like buggy whips and bustles,
Poetry's outlived its day.
Rhyme, like reason, doesn't pay.

Bards, ye'd now be to the Trade
As Pariahs. Ye would fade,
With the golden wealth ye minted,
Broke, unhonored, and unprinted!

"From Bard to Verse," Georgie Starbuck Galbraith: *Saturday Review*, 1952.

In the years between World War I and II eastern publishing houses published between ten and twenty volumes of verse a year. Even this modest flow of new poetry titles slackened to a mere dribble with the skyrocketing costs of paper and printing following World War II. One publisher estimated that his costs had risen 300 percent, and that this was true of all his colleagues.

Somehow this decreased output of poetry matched the climate of the reading public. Outside of a small elite, no one was reading it, and no one cared. Lamenting in a London verse magazine, the editors wrote:

What concerns us more particularly in this journal is the apparent lack of interest on the part of the public in poetry, or in *new* poetry, and the consequent disinclination of publishers to sponsor books of verse, about which there has been much discussion and lamentation of late. Certainly this is a serious state of affairs, which yet may prove a blessing in disguise if poets are prevented from rushing into print with sheaves of indifferent verse.*

One poet I know, typical of many, sent her manuscript during this trying decade to sixteen different publishers and received everything from perfunctory comments to raves. Several asked whether she had a novel in work. A novel, they suggested gently, might pay for the book of poems.

Poetry (London), Summer, 1951: edited by Richard March and Nicholas Moore.

She finally had an acceptance from the seventeenth on the list, a house of real prestige. The book was published and sold exactly 285 copies. The publisher lost a small shirt, and the poet gained a few good reviews. Who was right—the sixteen who saved their shirts, or the daring one who gave a chance to an unknown talent? It is certainly unfair to blame publishers for not wanting books that can sell only 285 copies. And I tried not to. Yet when asked why they published poetry at all, the publishers answered in a chorus, a trifle pious, "Because it is a cultural duty." It was at this point that I wondered. In an article in *The American Writer* Winfield Townley Scott queried:

> Since poetry represents the highest sort of literary ambition— a permanent contribution to literature—publishers allege it lends tone to their lists; they publish it for "prestige." I don't doubt them, but I think they also hope to have found the exceptional seller, and that this hope throws light on the frequency with which they cast off the young poet in short order. If "prestige" were all that was on their minds, why this "disappointment" about sales?*

Tiring of the New York runaround, I decided to try, at the suggestion of a friendly editor at *Poetry*, a Chicago house that had one or two good poets on its list, and was reportedly on the lookout for others. Here followed the first of two fascinating fiascoes that added nothing to my faith in my ultimate destiny, but which make good copy in retrospect.

After years of rejection letters, the opening letter from Editor Fred Wieck in January of 1954 was like an accolade, and I can repeat it almost word for word to this day. "If the publishing of poetry were a matter of quality and of nothing else, your volume would have found a publisher long ago. . . . But the other side to the publishing of poetry is the financial one. . . . Accordingly, we have sent your manuscript to our printers for an estimate. Would you object to paper covers? . . . I shall let you know our decision as promptly as it can be had."

Mr. Wieck's next letter was even more encouraging. He aske for another complete copy of the manuscript to send

'Poet or Peasant," Winfield Townley Scott: *The American Writer*, December 1952.

to Faber & Faber in London while they were waiting for the cost estimate from their own printers. "If our English colleagues think as highly of it as I do, and decide to share in an edition, the financial problem is solved."

I rushed off a carbon copy, and held my breath. Things were getting warm. Weeks and weeks went by. Nothing out of Chicago but an ominous silence. Finally on March 15 came a letter from another editor: "Mr. Wieck, with whom you have previously corresponded concerning the possible publication of the volume of your poems is no longer with us. . . . After consulting with our printers, I find that it would be practically impossible for us to produce an edition profitably. This is in no way a reflection on the poems themselves, since I find them of an extremely high caliber, and I only wish that the fate of poetry in the United States today allowed our publication."

I was right back where I started. No, not quite. I had a friend in Fred Wieck, though I didn't know where he was.

With nothing to lose, I sent the manuscript off to a book contest sponsored by Borestone Mountain Poetry Awards, in whose annual anthologies I had already appeared. I promptly forgot about it, but months later I was informed that in a competition of over two hundred entries I had won third place and had been given Honorable Mention.

This put a little starch in my ego, but did nothing to advance the cause of publication. I suppose I might have tried the Yale Series or The Lamont Poetry Selection sponsored by The Academy of American Poets. I would certainly have urged others to do so. But I didn't. Frankly, I was tired of the whole business, and decided to let the book lie in the bottom drawer. Like narcissus bulbs in the closet, perhaps it would sprout some blossoms if I left it alone.

Nor was I tempted in the least by the vanity publishers who continued to send me luring advertisements of their facilities, all couched in unctuous terms designed to disguise the fact that all they really wanted was my money regardless of the quality of the verse. In this discouraging postwar period more and more poets were resorting to subsidy. With enthusiasm for and confidence in their own work—

sometimes with real justification, but more often with none —they were digging into their pockets and paying $500 or more for what usually was called "partial" subsidy for a 500-run. Since in those days books of poetry only cost from 85 cents to $1.00 a copy to print, the vanity publisher had his money back without selling a copy. But the innocent poet seldom stopped to figure out the economics. After all, the poet argued, Edward Arlington Robinson did it. So did A. E. Housman. True enough, but it is unfortunately true that most books published at the poet's expense disclose not only vanity, but an appalling lack of talent. I believed then, as I believe now, that their effect on an unknowing public who cannot readily distinguish between a subsidized book and an unsubisidzed one must be seriously to dilute its response to poetry in general. I, for one, wanted no part of it. If my book were worth publishing at all, somebody else would underwrite the venture, not I. In the meantime I had great fun papering a wall in my bedroom with my collection of rejection slips, not just for the book manuscript, but for individual poems. They made a colorful montage, and as new ones came in, I added them with multicolored thumbtacks. Magazine acceptances were coming in during the same interval, so it never occured to me to be basically discouraged. I sometimes felt an enormous fatigue at having to put up with this delay any longer, but the faith never really faltered. A streak of iron, honestly come by, helped too. A friend of mine, showing another friend through my house, pointed out the wall of rejection slips and then, in a voice that was plainly meant to carry to the kitchen where I was preparing dinner, said, "Jeanie has the kind of ego that can stand it!"

In 1958 I tried again, this time to the only small press that seemed to be publishing good volumes of poems from new poets—Alan Swallow. Working out of Denver, he solved the problem of rising costs by doing almost all the work himself. "If I paid salaries or wages I couldn't afford to publish poetry." Swallow, however, was not sufficiently impressed with Burden to risk even that much, and the book went back into the bottom drawer.

During these years the *Zeitgeist* for poetry began to change. What was responsible for it as much as anything was the advent of paperbacks. At last the cost of publishing a book of poems was low enough to guarantee that the publisher would at least break even. Young people, particularly in colleges, found that poetry was within their budgets. Everyone knows how it flourished in coffee houses, on college campuses; how recordings of Dylan Thomas sparked a whole series of such; how suddenly the whole climate for the art changed from hostile or indifferent to almost popular.

Along with this warming up, of course, came more and more publishing houses into the act. Where a major house in New York had formerly dared to publish only one or two volumes of verse a year, it suddenly came out with six or eight, and some of them by relatively unknown poets. The university presses like Weslyan, Nebraska, Chicago, and Indiana (the latter had been in the forefront of this movement because of a large grant for the purpose) took courage and branched out into the unprofitable field of poetry.

Noting this, I sent my manuscript, retyped and improved by new poems, to the press of my alma mater, the University of Chicago. What followed is Fiasco No. 2, even more heartbreaking to me than the first. To make a long and tedious story short, after several exchanges of letters I was informed that the preliminary readers (outside of the editor-in-chief, who was in Europe) had been very favorably impressed. Furthermore, my corresponding editor enclosed a letter from an anonymous "outside reader" praising the book in such eloquent terms that I composed a letter immediately that began, "Dear Outside Reader: I love you." There was one reservation: O.R. had found four poems he thought "trailed off into rhetoric." Perhaps I should wait six months and substitute other poems for the weak ones? "However, if she gets huffy about that," he wrote, "I'd say publish it as it is. Its faults are those that afflict all poets; its virtues are the very big ones. She is already to me comparable with Kathleen Raine, and in a certain sharpness, superior to her."

I replied that of course I would do anything they suggested—drop the four poems entirely, or wait in the hopes
of writing others. My editor friend replied, "I want to mull
over this." I waited while he mulled. Weeks went by. Then,
on a morning I shall never forget, came a letter. The editor-
in-chief had returned from Europe. The University of
Chicago Press was not interested in publishing my book
then or ever. The letter was plainly written with personal
pain and embarrassment. I felt sorry for my corresponding
editor. He had not enjoyed writing that letter. The personal
letdown cannot be imagined. Nor could I understand how
a publisher could turn down a collection about which an
outside reader of their own choosing had written, ". . . this
is an immense, rare, possibly unique gift." I wept, but the
steel in my spirit acquired a new tensile strength.

From the experience I gained two important things: the
friendship of my corresponding editor, who wrote, "Be
sure to let me know when the book is published—as it surely
will be—so I can order a dozen copies for Christmas presents." And the knowledge that someone, I knew not who,
thought the manuscript was first-rate. To find out who
"outside reader" was took a bit of fancy detective work.
The University of Chicago Press was honor-bound not to
reveal his identity, though my editor friend promised to let
any other publisher to whom I sent the book know who he
was. It was two years and three publishers later that I dug
out the truth. By that time I had already guessed it.

One evening at a party in Los Angeles I was sitting on the
floor beside Oscar Williams, drinking red wine and munch-
ing rye bread and Camembert. He told me he had just signed
a contract with Clarke & Way, a new publishing house in
New York. I made a mental note and a few weeks later
looked them up. Sure enough, they were putting out some
beautiful books, most of them by new poets. Typography
was excellent; format, simple and in exquisite taste. What
could I lose but more postage? I wrapped up the book for
the eighteenth time and sent it off. One of Clarke & Way's
own outside readers was a poet whose work I knew well.

To him I sent O.R.'s remarkable evaluation, and to him the University of Chicago Press revealed his identity, as they had said they would. Clarke & Way's critic, it must be confessed, passed on the information to me. It was none other than poet and critic Howard Nemerov, in whose good graces I had never dreamed to be. It was almost reward enough for twelve years of waiting to know, even if secretly, that such a man as he thought I was "comparable with Kathleen Raine." I had never met him, nor had any prospect of doing so, but I knew his work and I was properly awed and grateful.

While I marinated in this lovely knowledge I could not share, months went by and no word out of Clarke & Way. To be accurate, *nine* months elapsed before I heard. Then on August 2, 1962 came a casual, if cordial, letter from David Way. I was standing in the kitchen when I read it, early one evening, and the first sentence brought the long journey to an end: "I don't know why it has taken me so long to tell you that we like your book and would like to publish it." The joy was both a balm and a wound. For days I told no one, scarcely able to believe it myself.

Months later in New York the book was given a "launching" party by Evelyn Ames at the Cosmopolitan Club, brilliant with champagne and bouquets of pink peonies and warm with the shared good wishes and affection of friends. One of those attending was Fred Wieck, now with Harper & Row. Though we had never met we recognized each other immediately. He came over with arms outstretched, gave me a short hug, bowed, and said with a broad smile, "This is the first time I have ever been invited to a literary party for *not* publishing a book!"

Afterward David Way and I walked down Fifth Avenue to look at the window display of *Naked as the Glass* in Scribner's bookstore. He took the pipe out of his mouth and jabbed me gently in the ribs with it. "Jean," he asked, "how in God's name did it take you so long to get published?"

"Well, David," I began, "it's a long story. . . ."

Chapter 4: Of Critics and Criticism

ONE OF THE REMARKS of George Dillon (former editor of *Poetry*) that I recall most vividly was one he made the first time I met him.

"I don't believe young poets need criticism as much as they need encouragement."

Being both very young and thin-skinned at the time, I was sure he was right. When I taught a poetry workshop many years later, I remembered those words and did my best to give both honest criticism *and* encouragement to the sensitive beginners—even if they had only a small talent.

But for the professional poet criticism is part of his lot, whether he likes it or not. It is both the price he pays for being published and a tribute to the fact that he is no longer an amateur.

I have been on both sides of the fence—what poet has not? I have reviewed books of poetry for magazines; I have given yards and yards of verbal criticism to students and fellow poets; and in turn I have been subjected to the critical scrutiny of some of the keenest minds in the field.

In general, literary criticism can be divided into two kinds: the rational, systematic kind that demands a highly trained, theoretical mind; and the more intuitive kind that disregards method and relies more on a long acquaintance with works of art and a responsiveness to them that is more emotional than intellectual. (I say *more*, not intending in any way to imply there is no rational or intellectual approach in the second category.)

Kenneth Burke is a good example of the first kind; James Dickey and Howard Nemerov of the second.

Of his own approach to criticism, Howard Nemerov has this to say:

Poetry and criticism are as a double star, and if we wish to go on in poetry beyond the first ecstatic stirrings of the imagination— which so often turn out to have been derivative, after all—we shall do well to learn all we can of what poetry is, and try to see by means of many examples how the art is constantly redefining itself. Studying one's contemporaries, one gets an idea of what is possible, as well as many ideas of what is not. . . .

Criticism, in whatever fancy dress, however, remains an art of opinion, and though the opinion should be supported by evidence, even that relation is a questionable one. Criticism is not knowledge, but neither ought it to be mystique, even if the sources of our opinions, and the influence of fashion upon these, are mysterious subjects. . . .

Critical method. To try not to have one. Or to have, at the most, two simple precepts: read what is in the poem; do not read what is not in the poem. . . . To be somewhat temperate, both in praising and damning. . . . Poetry and criticism stand quite properly as antagonists in what Blake calls "mental fight" and the "sports of the intellect," but the giant blows can hurt all the same. And we ought to err toward generosity, even though so many poems and so many novels offer the strongest temptation not to.*

This quotation provokes several comments:

There have in the recent past been two cases of criticism in print that did not "err toward generosity" and which aroused public indignation from poets and nonpoets alike. The first of course was the Ciardi-Lindbergh *cause célèbre* in *Saturday Review* in 1957. In this essay, written with fire and brimstone, Mr. Ciardi undertook to destroy Mrs. Lindbergh's status as a poet; it was in no sense merely a review of the book of poems in question. He had evidently stored up for years a repressed antipathy against certain kinds of women poets in general and Anne Lindbergh in particular. I remember reading the review with a kind of cold shock, not quite believing what I saw. When anger shows that plainly in a work of criticism, the critic, whether he knows it or not, has lost his argument. Ciardi was using a hatchet on a butterfly. If he felt the book was that bad, why didn't he just refuse to review it at all? In my opinion, such personal vitriol degrades the whole field of literary criticism. And yet when a friend questioned Ciardi about it afterward, he protested that it was not a personal attack and that he had not been angry!

Along with thousands of others, I wrote to Norman Cousins, Editor of *Saturday Review*, protesting this slugging of a fellow poet. For weeks and weeks the "Letters to the Editor" pages contained little but words pro and con the issue. Ciardi himself wrote a spirited answer to his detractors, "The Reviewer's Duty to Damn," backing down not at all. This merely fanned the bonfire. I was asked to speak on the subject before the Los Angeles P.E.N. Club. Shortly afterward I received a letter from George Dillon in which he said, "It would be interesting to see a transcript of your

*From Preface to *Poetry and Fiction* by Howard Nemerov: Rutgers University Press, 1963.

remarks on the Ciardi-Lindbergh brutalities. I read through the whole business last week, and it made me feel that I had lived beyond my time. I can't go along with calling the book contemptible or with most of the specific criticisms, which struck me as both pedantic and hysterical. A hangover in print."

Behind the scenes at the magazine, I understand, life was even more hectic. Not only were the mailbags heavier and more numerous than they had ever been before, requiring extra help to sort and answer, but the telephone was equally busy. Long distance calls from irate readers were put through at all hours, canceling subscriptions, and "Uncle Henry's Christmas gift subscription too!" They got Mr. Cousins up at one o'clock in the morning with calls from Colorado or California or someplace else in the West, apparently unaware of time differences, giving him the polls of their local literary societies. "We're twenty-two to four for Mrs. Lindbergh in Butte!" And Mr. Cousins would murmur a sleepy but polite "Thank you very much," and stumble back to bed.

That the whole controversy had its amusing side did not detract from the fact that the basic issue was anything but funny. Especially to Mrs. Lindbergh.

When a few years later, May Sarton took a similar drubbing in the *New York Times* at the hand of Karl Shapiro, I heard about it firsthand. While Mr. Shapiro's essay was not nearly as vicious as Mr. Ciardi's, his summation of Miss Sarton's collected poems, *Cloud, Stone, Sun and Vine*, was that, whatever her other literary gifts, she was a "bad poet." Considering Miss Sarton's enormous achievement as a poet and the critical approbation she had received here and abroad, Shapiro's words were hard to understand except on the basis of personal bias. Their reaction on Miss Sarton was as traumatic as might be expected. They were indeed "giant blows," and they hurt. When in a subsequent issue the *Times* printed indignant defenses from many of her colleagues, she may have felt better, but the wound was there for all time.

Is this the way to express critical disapproval? I have never thought so. Personal spite, value judgments that sound as though they were pronounced by God instead of submitted merely as opinion, vitriol that plainly shows through the lines—this is not criticism but merely letting off hostility. Perhaps the writer feels better afterward, but he has done no good to literature.

I recall an English professor at the University of Chicago who excelled in this sort of spiteful cleverness in grading papers. She was famous for such sneers in the margin as "You have a completely unwrinkled brain," and "Your vocabulary is mean and adolescent in the extreme, but quite adequate for the expression of your ideas." I think if she had ever written something like that on a paper of mine, I would never have written another word.

When it came time for me to pass judgment on my peers —and often my superiors—I tried to put into practice what I had learned. I found out that it was very easy to damn. (In fact, one way to gain immediate recognition as a critic is to lambaste every book one reviews.) There are surely more mediocre books of poetry published every year than good ones. And some are just plain awful. When I ran into one of the latter I sent it back, saying it was a waste of time for me or anyone to review it.

With the books for which I had respect, if not necessarily undiluted praise, I hit upon a somewhat novel, if simple, idea. It seemed to me that to give an honest appraisal of a book of poems one should know something about what the poet himself thinks of it. Was he happy with it? Did it say what he wanted it to say? For example, I had been asked by *Poetry* to review *More Clinical Sonnets* by Merrill Moore. I was no particular fan of Dr. Moore's, which was all the more reason I wanted to be fair to him. With this feeling strong in mind, I wrote to Dr. Moore in Boston and invited him to talk about his ninth book which had just been issued by Twayne Publishers. His reply was airmail, and enthusiastic:

How very unusual, and from my point of view, how very thoughtful of you. I am delighted to hear that *Poetry* asked you to do an article on my last book of clinical sonnets. . . . I think it's a slight improvement over *Clinical Sonnets*. I am happy to have this opportunity to unburden myself (pardon the pun), and explain to you that I got the idea of writing what I call "clinical sonnets" from E. A. Robinson. You are probably familiar with the sonnets in his collected poems (Macmillan) which he wrote between 1900 and 1935. They are pictures of people. I knew Mr. Robinson very well, from 1929 until his death in 1935, and we talked over poetry quite a lot. He helped me form my style, I think, and as I have written in the past 35 years I think I know increasingly what I want to do. I try to present pictures of people as people, somewhat realistically, sometimes symbolically, sometimes casually, sometimes even flippantly, people have said. That is what I am trying to do. How well I have done it you can decide better than I.

With these clues at hand, I went back to a study of Edward Arlington Robinson's poetry as a guide to an analysis of Dr. Moore's. Now let us see what I did with it. (Incidentally, I prefaced my criticism with a story of my letter to Moore and his reply.) Excerpts from my review follow:

Re-reading Robinson's sonnets proved to be a pleasant and illuminating task. The similarity to Moore's verse is immediately apparent. So are the divergencies. Robinson was not a psychiatrist like Dr. Moore, yet his delineations are generally more profound. Moore, on the other hand, has a refreshing liveliness and wit that the somber Robinson seems to lack. Moore is often impudent, sometimes biting in his portrayals; Robinson is gentler. Moore loves to caricature, while Robinson gives more of the third dimension.

Both poets, however, are interested in people as people. Neither moralizes. Such detachment makes for accuracy and a vividness that needs no graphic illustrations. Being of the opinion that verse should stand alone—that if it is good it needs no picturing, and if it isn't no illustration will help it—I regret the Edward Gorey illustrations of Dr. Moore's book. For me, they distract from rather than enhance the poems, and give the erroneous impression that this is a book solely of light verse.

Both poets, too, like the speech rhythms, the easy vernacular of their own time and place. Dr. Moore writes, "I wouldn't say that I am an 'intellectual poet.' More I would say that I am a lyrical poet and I myself believe poetry should contain considerable 'communication,' if not 'transport.' " There can be no doubt of Moore's communication. His is the abrupt attack, the rushing in on a subject without knocking, the equally swift withdrawal. His character sketches are drawn in plain terms; there are never any unnecessary frills. Even of metaphor he is shy. He does not seem to be fascinated by words as such. Language, commonly one of the chief preoccupations of a poet, concerns him only moderately. His lines are clean, economical, tight. Often this understatement makes for low-key drama; sometimes it sinks to the banal and prosey. . . .

Devoid of any literary cultism, spontaneously and vigorously, Merrill Moore does, for the most part, accomplish what he set out to do. His people are always memorable. Sometimes one wishes he were not in such a hurry, that he would round out his men and women a little more. But perhaps we are asking too much. After all, this scientist-poet said "somewhat realistically." For even the most casual reader there is wonderful wry fun here. There are also the poignance and penetration of a serious poet.*

While I have omitted from the excerpt above all quotations from Dr. Moore's work (and I used several), it is plain to see that my prior querying of the poet did not in any way lessen my own objectivity nor dull my critical sense. Nor was it just a courteous gesture. What it did do was to force my analytical thinking to include and evaluate his own point of view, which is surely as relevant as my own. I was rewarded when, after the review appeared in *Poetry*, a critic-poet of far wider experience than my own wrote me, saying that in his opinion mine was the only review in the magazine that reviewed the *book* instead of serving as an outlet for the critic's own pet theories or peeves.

Another example illustrates this even more pointedly. *Prairie Schooner* sent me for review Howard Moss's *A Winter Come, a Summer Gone*, then just published by Scribner's. Again I decided to find out from Mr. Moss what his own attitudes toward his poetry were, and again I was rewarded by candor, insight, humor, and great good sense. ("What I would like best is to write like Shakespeare. If you put anything like that in your review, I'll kill you. . . . More and

*Quoted from *Poetry*, April 1954, Copyright by the Modern Poetry Association, by permission of the editor.

more, I try not to falsify emotions, not to settle for less than the exact descriptive equivalent of a feeling, as well as of objective things. . . . I think one of the major problems in a poem is tone, that is consistency of style, feeling, etc. . . . In short, again, a truly good poem strikes me as one which has eliminated the irrelevant. . . . I think the whole business of the beats vs. the elegants, however, is a lot of nonsense. You don't have to hate Hopkins to like Whitman, and part of the stupidity of it comes from people who are dying to make poetry 'American.' To me, it has always been inter-national.")

There was a great deal more, all of it enlightening and stimulating, and prompted by it, I read the poems for the ninth or tenth time with wider eyes. My review, briefly quoted, follows, and I quote from it in defense of this kind of preparation for criticism. I do not mean to imply that it is the *only* kind, but it can be extremely helpful.

. . . Mr. Moss's audience is probably not as wide as it should be, though there is nothing of the eccentric in these poems. They are formal, seasoned, spare but not ascetic, controlled. Their emotions are reined in; their diction elegant but muscular. They poke at the surfaces of things with wit and irony ("Horror Movie," "Tourists," "Florida") and probe with seriousness and a cutting edge both the depths of his own unconscious and the swampy places of the human predicament.

Moss, himself, dislikes "raw" poetry, poetry that "shouts." In his own work he never raises his voice. Within this somewhat limited register, however, he has managed amazing variety, subtle tensions of sound and meaning, and given us insights that excite and kindle.

Moss brings to his themes (love, the search for identity, the futility of attempted communication, time, loneliness) an unusually deft technical skill as well as a sensitive and civilized imagination. . . . While I question some of his rhymes, his rhythms are as taut and personal as his speech. He is perhaps overly fond of trimeter, but it is a small fault. His imagery is both precise and catholic. . . . Sometimes as in "Dreams" I have wished that it were still more exact, even at the expense of being less musical. Mr. Moss's "pitch," it must be added, is always absolute. . . .

One cannot fail to recognize, however, that his deep love of language . . . is also his greatest pitfall. His delight in playing with words sometimes leads him not only into mere decoration, but into such conceits as "And harp on the harpings of themselves . . ." and "The leaves' leavetaking overtaking leaves." Also, his fondness for repeating words in the same line occasionally becomes a mannerism: "Burn, they burn to say"; "But lie to me, lie next to me"; "But nightly at our trades / Of reeling in the real / The figures seem too real. . . ."

. . . because the questions he asks are all fundamental, hence capable of no final conclusion, we come away not with answers, but with a reawakened sense of the profound importance of the query. This, of course, is a matter of the delicate dance of theme *and* form. On this Mr. Moss says, "I think a poem should be strategic in the sense that a form is being constructed and that the interplay of that form with what is being said must finally mesh into something which has no irrelevancies. . . . What I would like to do is to write poems, each one of which contains a small but complete world in itself." That he accomplishes this over and over is no small feat. . . .*

Some reviewers seem to ignore the simple truism that because of their own personal philosophical or psychological orientation—their own temperament—not all poetry is going to be equally pleasing to them, *even if it is of equal merit.* For an editor to assign a book of way-out poetry to a poet-critic whose own work is on a completely different and more conservative wavelength (or vice versa) is to run the risk of getting in return an unconsciously biased review. I can think of several poets writing today whose work I would not dream of criticizing, because it is outside my own frame of reference to such an extraordinary degree that I could not possibly do it justice. They simply do not speak to me at all. But I do not say, in print or otherwise, *these are bad poets.*

This whole problem of the editorial ethic received a go-around in *Saturday Review* a few years ago to which several poets and critics contributed opinions and reactions, many of them similar to my own. I still cringe when I read criticism

*Reprinted from *Prairie Schooner*: copyright 1961 by the University of Nebraska Press.

of prose or poetry that is obviously prejudiced, not by the quality or lack of it in the work at hand, but by a blind spot in the critic's own eye. We all have them. We are rugged individualists, not Olympian sages. We have our strong likes and dislikes. But, in my opinion, print is no place to air them except with strong reservations. There are many kinds of excellence—not just one.

If I may be permitted a personal aside, an example of this was brought out by a striking contrast in reviews of my own book. Of the twenty reviews I read (and there may have been others, as I did not have a clipping bureau), eighteen were laudatory, one so-so, and one harsh. The latter, by a highly respected woman poet, shredded the book to confetti by being severely critical of the very things that others had praised. While Howard Nemerov had said, for instance, that "her handling of the line, if there were nothing else, shows a near absolute tact," this critic insisted that I lacked "an instinct for what the line is." James Dickey had said, "She has the right instinctive feel of language"; in contrast, this reviewer said I had no instinctive rapport with language. And while Hayden Carruth said, "She has kept her symbols clean and intellectually hard, without sacrificing any warmth of feeling," my detractor felt that "being careful to exclude all that is coarse, uncertain, 'ugly,' she arrives mainly at an anemic refinement."

Every publishing poet could point to equally wide variances in critical reception, and I only cite my own because the evidence is more easily accessible. Strange as it may seem, I prize that unfavorable review today. It taught me a great deal, even though it strikes me as being not wholly accurate.

It would be nice to believe only the praise, but I am inclined to think that in many instances both kinds of opinion are, in part, correct—the pro and the con. But more correct as opinion than as absolute aesthetic judgment. The absolutes will take time to prove correct, and even time is fickle. Consensus seems to dictate a small range of art as Good (white), and a somewhat larger range as Bad (black), but the wide area in between is just various shades of gray, and the best critics in the world are stumbling around in it, trying to find their way.

A word about dust jacket puffery. Prepublication endorsement on book jackets by fellow poets is a practice easily overdone, though as a reader I am always interested in what other poets think of a book. I may or may not agree with them, but I confess I find their remarks provocative. Some critics when reviewing a volume whose back cover is liberally plastered with encomiums, automatically indulge in the opposite. The more prominent the poets quoted in tribute, the more severe the criticism. It becomes a kind of reverse status symbol to be in open disagreement with the top literary echelon. Anyone who doubts this should drop in on any literary cocktail party and listen to the lively discussion of who had dared to spit in whose eye in the *Yale Review* or last Sunday's *Herald Tribune*. And there are always some who traffic in trying to destroy any well-established literary hero or heroine. ("Really, you know, Robert Frost is terribly tedious at times, don't you think?")

In the last analysis, neither the applause nor the boos are very important. One must ultimately divest oneself of all of it and go back to the lonely and difficult business of writing more poems. That what one has written out of a solitary agony of spirit has meant something to someone else is a grace, but it has nothing to do with why one writes poetry. One writes to keep alive a self that would wither away without it.

Chapter 5: Poetry as a Platform Art

ON THE BACK COVER of *Poetry* every month there used to appear a quotation from Whitman to the effect that to have great poetry one must have great audiences too.

After several years of reading before groups of all kinds, and having just returned from a tour of colleges and universities of the Pacific Northwest, I can report that as far as audiences are concerned, Whitman has nothing to worry about.

Along with politics, religion, and the problem of identity in modern society, poetry is a very live issue.

Today poets are frequently members of the faculty as poets-in-residence (a title that usually means the status of lecturer, and is for one year) or, if they have sufficient achievement and/or degrees, as permanent professors of English. Furthermore, visiting poets are invited to read on campus for fees that range all the way from $50 to $1,500. Provided a poet can group several of these engagements within a small traveling radius, he can net enough to make the trip worthwhile. To aid in this effort, the Academy of American Poets has recently set up regional poetry circuits whereby a poet may be booked for a group of colleges in a certain area—the Midwest, the Northeast, the Northwest, etc.—and be guaranteed a sum sufficient to give him a small profit over his not inconsiderable expenses—the cost shared equally by the institutions involved. This has proved a very happy solution, both for the poets and the campus lecture bureaus.

These readings are not infrequent esoteric events confined to the anterooms of college life but are a prominent part of the current lecture series, widely publicized on campus by posters and newspaper stories. The event is not only announced in English classes but is promoted by student committees who plan coffee hours with the poet, luncheons, teas, discussions. Poetry workshops often invite the visitor to drop in on their classes. On my recent tour I talked informally with two honors classes and thoroughly enjoyed the give and take. At another college I gave personal interviews at twenty-minute intervals to students desiring private criticism of their poems.

All this is in striking contrast with poetry at colleges and universities twenty-five years ago. And nobody knows better than I. I was there.

When I was in college, art exhibits did a lively student business. Musicians played to full houses. Lecturers on anthropology or political science, no matter how dull, drew crowds. Poets were unheard of.

58

Furthermore, there was not a single class in the writing of poetry, no workshops on or off campus, few if any professors who cared to teach anything past Browning and Matthew Arnold. The only encouragement I received for the poetry I was trying to write came from Thornton Wilder in private sessions outside of class. How starved I was for the kind of help such an artist can give—not only criticism, invaluable as this can be, but the contagion of enthusiasm for the art itself that can only be communicated by someone actively engaged in and committed to it—is attested by the fact that I have never forgotten anything he said to me. Not only did he disparage mediocrity and sentimentality at a time in life when one is most susceptible to them ("Don't waste your superlatives on the almost great and the near-beautiful!" he would storm. "Otherwise you'll have nothing left when you hear the Bach B-Minor Mass!"), but over and over he gave me the kind of advice that is much more important than where to place the rhyme or how to break up the monotony of iambic pentameter. I dropped all the little bits and pieces of his wisdom into a basket, and today they read something like this:

> Don't be afraid of aloneness, for poetry is born of aloneness. Be obsessed of your own calling. Do not fear to make a mistake, a great mistake, a lifetime mistake. Be a little in love with heresies. Be a world to yourself. Be humble, and above all, be patient. Do not stop writing poems; do not stop, no matter what.

I have often quoted Mr. Wilder for audiences of young people and his words seem as fresh today as they did then. And as difficult. But students today don't need or want the easy answer, whether they are aiming to be nuclear physicists or poets. And perhaps these two disparate groups need each other more than we know. I once spoke to the combined English classes at the California Institute of Technology and found them as vitally concerned with modern poetry and their own relationship to it as they were with the latest shot at the moon. In my tour of the Northwest I was surprised to find science and math majors as well as those from psychology and economics flocking to the readings and even their professors dropping in without apologies. I cannot imagine this happening at the University of Chicago in the thirties and forties, though I am sure it is a commonplace today.

Along with live readings of poetry, recordings and tapes are in wide demand on campuses and elsewhere. FM radio and even occasionally TV feature poetry readings, and the resulting mail, while not rivaling Batman's, is respectable and enthusiastic. The general public, one might assume, is learning what audiences in the more remote past took for granted: that poetry read to oneself from a book is only half the story. To hear poetry read aloud is the other half, and another experience entirely.

Some of these records and tapes are by the poets themselves, some by well-known actors and actresses. It is a toss-up who does the better job, though other things being equal I would rather hear the poet read his own work than the most skillful professional. What would be our richness today if we could hear Shakespeare read "Hamlet"—even if he were not as good as one of his leading men? Others come to mind: Rilke reading the Duino Elegies; Shelley with his "Ode to the West Wind"; Matthew Arnold interpreting "Dover Beach."

Today we are fortunate enough to have poets like Robert Lowell and W. S. Merwin adding their own personal dimensions to their powerful poems; Howard Nemerov speaking his poems in a gentle, almost hypnotic chant; John Crowe Ransom, reading as only he could, with an elegant, precise diction his elegant and precise verse—to mention only a few of hundreds available to us today. Greatest of all, of course, was Dylan Thomas, who was probably responsible as much as any poet for the sudden popularity of recorded poetry, who sang, intoned, and organ-boomed his poems like the wild Welsh bard he was.

Each gives us something personal and private, above and beyond the words themselves. Only the poet himself knows precisely where to place the emphasis, how to manipulate

60

the cadences, when to raise or lower the tension. So, while I have heard many highly skilled actors read poetry—and even poets read other poets very well indeed (Nemerov reading Wallace Stevens is a good example)—I vote for the poet reading his own.

While I learned from an actress how to project my voice, and how to keep the wistfulness out of it ("You sound droopy, dammit, and your poems are strong. Speak out directly!"), I still probably do not read as she would prefer. My defense is that I read them as I want them to sound. I have listened to myself on tape enough to know by now what to avoid and, I hope, what to make the most of. Some poets I have heard throw their poems away. They mumble to their lecterns. This is frequently (or perhaps always) the result of a feeling of inferiority that the poet is not even aware of. But it shows unmistakably in his voice. One must read as though one thought the poems superb—even if one knows full well that they will always be less than what one meant them to be.

I think perhaps I myself am learning with experience something about this art of reading poetry aloud, because over and over I hear, "Your voice fits the poems perfectly" or "You sound the way the poems read." If that is true, that is what I am after. No more, no less.

What are audiences seeking when they come to a reading of poetry?

I suppose the same things they seek when they attend an exhibit of T'ang Dynasty art, or a Segovia concert, or wander through the sculpture garden at the Museum of Modern Art. They hope, quite simply. for aesthetic pleasure in seeing the old re-created in the new, for intellectual nourishment, for emotional release. And, at least in the case of college students, for something more than that. In this perilous age of ours, art, even more than religion, seems to offer young people today a reaffirmation of the only values they can be sure of. Perhaps this is one reason why poetry has come so astonishingly alive on American campuses across the land; why it is argued about, discussed, fought over; why students flock to readings to sit in rapt attention to the last word; why they line up to buy books of poetry as though they were going out of print the next day.

On the occasions I have given personal interviews to student poets, I have had more appointments than I could possibly handle. Some of the poems showed sprigs of talent; some were extraordinary; most were dreadful. But the poetry was not the only important object at hand. What these young people wanted to talk about was themselves— the direction of their longings, their confusions, the hurt and empty places of their spirits. The poetry was the vehicle. Through it they reached out for some kind of meaning.

In a curious way, I think the same thing applies to those in the audience who never wrote a line and who came to listen for reasons they themselves did not quite understand. If poetry, no matter how personal, plumbs deep enough, it will take others there too—into the great common sea that nourishes us all. In our too-busy world there is little enough of that kind of experience. We are deafened by society's platitudes. Each of us has private feasts he does not know how to celebrate. Each of us is more crucified than he knows. Poetry—all art—is one of the ways in which we bear the burden of our common paradox, not by giving easy answers, but by offering magic and transcendence in the light of which birth and death, love and loss, seem two halves of a whole. In poetry truth and experience become one.

Incidentally, the amount of pure feeling generated by a reading of poetry is not inconsiderable. Many poets have commented on it—how the room seems to become choked with it, how sudden, unexpected bursts of applause will sometimes release it, or equally surprising explosions of laughter. Often there are tears, not, as one girl explained, because the poems were sad, but because "I haven't been stirred up at that depth in years and years."

If someone ever asked—and no one did—what I thought was the most important result of poetry readings, especially for young people, I would reply that it was possibly none of the things I had previously mentioned, significant as they might be. I would have recalled vividly my own troubled ecstasy the first time I heard Robert Frost read his own poems, the first experience of hearing "Fern Hill" on record, the initial excitement of listening to "Ash Wednesday" and "Anna Livia Plurabelle" in the original—and how such experiences kindled my own imagination. This, in the last analysis, is the great gift. The artist in any medium exercises an inductive influence. He stirs up our own original thinking. The greatest compliment I ever received for one of my own readings—imperfect and limited as it always is—was overhearing a boy who had been too shy even to shake hands shout to a friend as he dove up the aisle, "Wow! I'm going home and write a poem!"

Part II: *As Editor*

Chapter 6: *They Get Madder in Maine*

BY FAR the most controversial hat I wear is that of Poetry Editor. As a poet one seldom if ever hears from one's public. Indeed, one sometimes wonders whether such a public actually exists. The fan mail I have accumulated over more than twenty years of seeing my own poetry in print fits easily into one file folder and the bulge is barely noticeable. Teachers occasionally receive mail, but in general they are given their praise or blame verbally.

But as a nonresident editor of a poetry page in a New England magazine (the national circulation of which is a surprising 225,000 plus), I can testify that not all the mail one receives is manuscripts. A sizable share of it is the foaming personal opinion of one's readers. While compliments are not infrequent (and doubly treasured), it is the adrenalin of outrage that impels most of the correspondents. If you think that readers of poetry are droopy old men putting themselves to sleep after a hard day, or starry-eyed adolescents in search of a quotation for their valentines, you are badly mistaken. They are teachers, housewives, college professors, farmers, children, engineers, other editors, artists, advertising executives, prisoners, and a miscellaneous assortment of members of local poetry societies. I have received letters—both pro and con—from every region of the country, but by far the largest proportion naturally comes from New England, and of that group the angriest are, for some reason, from Maine. I find it hard to understand, I confess, why some readers get so exercised about one page in a magazine that boasts more than a hundred an issue. If they don't like it why don't they just turn it over, snarl a little, and go on to something they do like.

Since these letters of criticism promise some enlightenment for readers as well as writers of poetry, it is from them that I shall quote.

The panning can be divided roughly into two kinds:

1. Accusations of personal bias based on the fact that the writers' own poems were not accepted for publication.

2. Invective against my taste in poetry and instructions for its improvement.

These are, of course, not peculiar to me. All poetry editors receive them and, after a minimal exposure, are impervious to them. No editor worth his salt can do anything less than trust his own judgment, faulty as that may be. It is precisely because of that judgment that he was hired for the job. Until he is replaced he must abide by it.

The first kind of brickbat—the personal attack—is in the minority. Most verse writers, if they have been around for

65

even a short time, get used to rejection slips. As one becomes more and more sure of oneself, one learns objectivity, how to take suggestion and criticism, even the more blunt "That's just not good!" as impersonal comment. Editors find that in general the more mediocre the talent, the greater the vanity. And when vanity is hurt, letter-writing is apt to begin.

A juicy example of this arrived one day at *Yankee* headquarters, addressed to Mr. Sagendorph, the editor, from an irate gentleman who had just returned from a writers' conference in—guess where?—Maine. The gist of his communication (and wrath) was that someone at the conference had confided that I would accept no manuscript from a poet whose book had been published by a certain vanity publishing house because I had once had a manuscript turned down by them! Furthermore, the writer went on, he now knew why his own poems had not made the grade with me, since he himself had had a book put out by this house. Since he had had poems accepted by other magazines (listed), obviously he was not being rejected on *literary* grounds, but only because of the pet peeve of the poetry editor. Surely Mr. Sagendorph would want to right this grave injustice.

By return mail Mr. Sagendorph called the charges "ridiculous" and "gross libel." With my own reply I took careful aim. If the charges had not been so slanderous, they would have been hilarious, but I could not let an accusation against my integrity as an editor go unanswered. My standards of taste anyone is free to question, but not my honesty. Because this man's letter also displays an ignorance of how poetry editors work, I would like to delineate briefly on my reply.

That a many-times-rejected poet should think that an editor has some kind of personal grievance against him, that he lies awake at night dreaming up ways to thwart his literary career, is just so much nonsense. It probably came as a shock to my correspondent from Maine that *I did not even know his name*, much less the name of his book or its publisher. (And of course I never in my life submitted a manuscript to them or to any vanity publisher.) He could send me poems every month and I still wouldn't remember him. As I explained to him, I read hundreds of poems every week, fifty-two weeks a year, and have been doing so for over ten years. I couldn't repeat the name of a single rejected poet in the whole lot. My only interest is in the *poem*. If it attracts me I look to see who wrote it. Otherwise I pay no attention whatever to the name at the top of the page. It simply goes back into the return envelope, and I pick up the next one. This is true of every poetry editor I ever knew. In the first place, there is no time to memorize names of unsuccessful poets—they comprise 99.9 percent of our mail. In the second place, we don't care about names. Our attitude is totally impersonal. I neither care who the poet is, nor where he came from, nor where he was published before. I don't care if he is well known or if this is his first poem. I have published both famous names and unknowns. I repeat, all I care about is the poem and whether or not it satisfies my taste for excellence. A good poem will always find a welcome; an unsuccessful poem will always go back. It is as simple—and as complicated—as that.

The second category of diatribe is the fatter file. The criticisms may all be boiled down to the simple query, "Why do you pay money for all that modern, meaningless verse when you could reprint 'Hiawatha' for nothing?" These are the readers who criticize any poetry editor for not printing the kind of verse they memorized in grade school. Most of it probably wasn't very good even then, but it is far less so now. Poetry, like any art, belongs to its time as well as to all time. To criticize poetry because it is too "modern" (as many of these correspondents do) is simply no criticism at all.

I never answer this kind of letter. This is not out of disrespect for the writer's opinion—he is certainly in the majority if nothing else—but because nothing I could say would change his point of view one whit, and as John Ciardi once remarked, it is the kind of difference of opinion that splits the poetry-reading public right down the middle.

Let me quote from a few such heated communications:

"Why not some of the real old favorites? 'oft in the stilly night / E're slumbers chain has bound me . . .' "

"Is that stuff you print month after month and call poetry meant for a joke? I realize there is some beauty in the abstruse but why is the moon poor in 'Haiku'? Please, just part of the time, give the lovers of plain old everyday poetry a chance."

"One reason I subscribed for your magazine was that I like poetry, but the stuff you print now I have been unable to find one person who likes it. There is no beauty, no sense, or anything else to it. All I can see is people who have missed the nicer things in life. So please cancel my subscription." (From Maine, naturally.)

"What is happening to the Poetry Page of *Yankee*? . . . That trash would fit better in Greenwich Village than in New England. Your editor should print not her peculiar taste, but what the subscribers like and pay for."

(To a similar complaint, Mr. Sagendorph once replied: "The readership of our magazine is made up of very many different kinds of people and some of them, I think you must realize, like the worst verse in the world better than they do the best poetry in the world. It is not our intention to cater to the ones who like the worst verse—of this you may be sure.")

One woman said my poetry better fitted the pages of an academic quarterly. She meant it as a slap, but I was flattered. While I could not print as "highbrow" or cerebral poetry as, say, *The Kenyon Review*—it would not fit as homespun a magazine as *Yankee*—I could choose high-quality verse without regard for its regionalism.

What kind of poetry do these critics really want?

They want the kind that fits their psyches in the same way a nice warm, worn, saggy armchair fits their tired bones.

Real poetry, on the other hand, is always something of a hair shirt. It is not comfortable. It is slightly abrasive; it is always exhilarating.

". . . the kind of poetry in today's magazines and publications are nothing but conundrums. All of this high flown conglomeration of words and pretty phrases that reflect only the ego of the writer surely is the reason why the reading public no longer enjoys poetry. The great treasures still loved are the simple understandable messages such as were written by Longfellow, Edgar Guest, Whittier, Field . . ." writes one correspondent from Massachusetts, typical of many.

If a poetry editor published what this man—and many others—want, he would be publishing nothing but bad poetry. And if poetry editors are not authorities on anything else they are surely experts on Bad Poetry.

Most Bad Poetry can be divided into four categories:

1. *Pornography.* Only recently I rejected a wad of erotic verse that would have done credit to Henry Miller. My only concern was that I might be arrested for sending such stuff *back* through the mail. This kind of verse is rather rare, but the general public might be surprised to know it exists to any degree at all. (I have never been able to determine in my own mind whether the poet really thinks this is worth publishing, or whether it is merely a form of literary masturbation.)

2. *The Love Burble.* This is the largest category, by far. The joys of first love, the agonies of unrequited—these would fill several wastebaskets a week. While a *good* love poem is a joy forever, the not-so-good-to-downright-poor ones flood the mail and turn the stomach. Most poets *begin* by writing love poems—and not unnaturally so—but if one continues to write nothing else, one's literary development at least has been sadly arrested. Once I took the liberty of calling to the attention of a contributor that she was sending me nothing but poems of the "he doesn't love me any more and oh the pain of it" variety, and that she was in a rut. Next time she sent me four poems on other subjects, one of which was good enough to accept. Her accompanying letter expressed profound gratitude for calling this to her attention.

3. *The Intellectualoid Mutter.* These are the poems (sometimes bad imitations of Eliot) written not out of an honest

desire to experiment, but out of a kind of exhibitionism. ("Look how many Italian, Greek and Hebrew references I can bring in! Look how many polysyllabic words I know! See how many wild metaphors I can flap about!") These may speak to the poet, but not to anyone else. The ostentatiously obscure poem is as bad as the cliché-ridden sonnet —but for opposite reasons.

4. *The Pious Peep*. The second largest group of failures is the so-called devotional poem. To the person with honest religious feeling (whether orthodox or unorthodox) they are, more often than not, acutely painful. Even more difficult than expressing love for another human being is to couch in original terms one's love for God. Not impossible but, admittedly, very hard to do well.

Cutting across these four groups, one can sort out certain common faults:

1. *Tired language*. The poet is using worn-out imagery— poetic nouns bolstered by equally exhausted adjectives. Too many adjectives is probably the commonest fault of all. If the nouns are strong they need a minimum of support. This is equally true of verbs and adverbs.

2. *Generalizations*. Too many poets *talk about* a subject rather than re-create it. They indulge in windy generalizations about Life and the World, about Love and Nature, instead of giving us a vivid personal experience.

3. *Naive Insights*. Perhaps the basic failure of any poem is a failure of insight. If in a poem one has seen to only a shallow depth, no amount of technical skill will save it. As a matter of fact, the commonest failures are not technical at all. (Oddly enough, all poetry editors complain that 90 percent of the bad poetry submitted is in perfect sonnet form.)

4. *No Feeling for Form*. Form in its widest sense is at least half the poem. Perhaps more. It encompasses not only rhythm, rhyme (or lack of it), but the subtleties of language and sound, the cadence, beat, *tension* of a poem. This is not superimposed from without, but grows from within. Every poem brings its own architecture with the first line. It is part of the total concept of the poem. One follows it; and because

it is largely intuitive, it is always hard to explain to the neophyte.

5. *Self-expression Instead of Urgency.* I do not see how a good poem can be written out of anything but a sense of urgency. Bad poems often display either too much urgency (emotion let off like steam), or too little. The difference between these faults is both a hairline distinction and infinities of space. The "too little" fault results in imitations of poems. They are not finished because in a very real sense they have never begun.

6. *In Summary, Copycatness.* Clichés, not only of words but of attitudes, fill the mailbag, ruin most of the poems. Would-be poets imitate and echo, imitate and echo—and not the masters of the art, but the most mediocre prototypes, the poesy-writers who were not even good in the original. True poetry is an encounter within oneself between one's life and one's death. It involves all one's values, not just literary ones. It is never imitative. It is as new and old, as wonderful and ordinary, as tomorrow morning.

Poets need never worry that a successful poem will ever get away. It is too rare. If anything *approaching* success lands on my desk I am grateful. Sometimes a poem will be weak in only one stanza or one line. Though I understand few editors have time for this, the teacher in me can't let it go without a note suggesting revision. Never have I received anything but gratitude from the poet. Gratitude and hard work. Six or seven revisions have sometimes gone back and forth between us before the poem is right. Once in a while the poem breaks apart in the reworking and can't be saved. I am as sorry as the poet.

On the other hand, many poets *ask* for personal criticism when they submit their manuscripts. No poetry editor has time for this; we would be doing little else. Neither do we have time to explain to the poet what kind of poetry we publish. The poet should be able to determine our criteria by his own efforts.

I do admit to having a few pet peeves:

1. No stamped, self-addressed envelope. The only manu-

scripts I return without envelopes are those from children, elderly people, and prisoners. The rest are destroyed.

2. Stamps but no envelope. This means I must stop, find an envelope, and address it. With hundreds of poems to read, this is unnecessarily time-consuming.

3. Oversized envelopes. These are a darn nuisance. No poem receives better treatment because it arrives flat with fancy cardboard backing. It merely looks pretentious. Use ordinary No. 10 envelopes, folding the poems to fit, and enclose another No. 10 envelope folded twice. A return envelope of dinky proportions that must take a dozen sheets of bond paper guarantees that the returned poems will be in a deplorable state (usually blamed on the editor).

4. Carbon copies (I never read them); dog-eared copies; hand-written copies.

5. Poems accompanied by photographs, publishers' blurbs of their vanity books, current lecture schedules, or local newspaper clippings of other poems.

What is it then that we look for and so seldom find? What *is* poetry? I have likened it to a child's kaleidoscope— hundreds of different-colored elements of reality, caught by a frame, an artifice, a form, into patterns. The pieces themselves are rough and sharp to the touch. Not soft and pretty. They are constantly shifting and shimmering, for poetry is a dynamic thing. Every time you look at a true poem it is different. But the form and the pattern hold. It is naive and childlike and sophisticated and subtle and true. It is serious without being solemn; it is profound without being pompous. As Charles Morgan says in *Sparkenbroke*, ". . . art was the most profound of all the intimations of immortality. Beneath the impact of a work of art . . . we undergo a kind of conversion. Our stiffness breaks, we flow again; we are aware, as at no other time, of a continuity in ourselves, as though we were given eyes to look up and down the river far beyond the little section of it that is our life in this world."

Chapter 7: The Radical Right—Even in Poetry

SINCE ALL LETTERS addressed to me at the magazine must first go across the editor-in-chief's desk, they occasionally get to me with a scrawled marginal note from him to the effect that he has not answered it, and that I may or may not as I see fit. Occasionally he will write, "I answered this, so help me, God!"

One of those I did take time to answer was inspired by a poem of Hildegarde Flanner's in our Christmas issue—a poem I considered one of the loveliest I had ever received. Every poetry editor knows how difficult it is to get unusual, fresh insight in poems on a subject as overdone as Christmas. Miss Flanner's poem is here reprinted intact:

WOMAN AND CHILD IN STONE

Our Lady, have you not heard the rumour
    that we are lost?
You, with your Gothic and dovelike hands
    Forever crossed
In a darling cradle for your Son,
You, with your half-Oriental eyes
    Peaceward and upward toward Paradise—
Mother, Mother, are you not aware
There is neither Peace nor Paradise anywhere?
For the sad and iniquitous,
The scorners at your knee,
The violent and the savage,
The free and the unfree
    One Saviour alone will not suffice.
    Must He, the Prince of Anguish, be
      crucified twice?
Mary, Mary,
    Because of the gruesome and terrible burden of love
    We lay on your only Son,
For His sake, Mary,
    Give us another One.

From *Yankee*, December 1962.

Two months later came the following letter from a member of the Poetry Right—closely allied in attitude and technique with the Political Right:

Editors of Yankee Magazine—Unfortunately I have only just read the December Yankee else I would have written before this. I am not only surprised but deeply shocked at a supposedly New England publication stooping to sacrilege.

"Woman and Child in Stone" by Hildegarde Flanner is an affront to all Christians and completely in error.

While the Virgin Mary did indeed give the Saviour birth He was God given and He fulfilled His mission of Redemption for all who will believe in Him. To suggest anything else, or that "One

Saviour alone will not suffice" is blasphemy and if you did not know it *you do now*!

I expect a public apology to those who come of a long line of Yankees who settled this country— *your readers* "for ye glorie of God and advancement of ye Christian faith."

This time I had no alternative of silence. I rolled up my sleeves, sharpened my pencil, and replied:

DEAR MRS. . . .

In reply to your letter of February 18 which was referred to me, may I say that it is I who am shocked. It would never occur to me that anyone could possibly be offended by Miss Flanner's beautiful and reverent poem. As a matter of fact, it evoked more letters of praise than any poem we ever published. Our readers come from every state in the Union and every shade of religious opinion— yours was the only protest.

But the issue raised by your letter is much more important and profound than one poem.

We at *Yankee* (and I know this holds true of other magazines as well, other than those supported by a particular denomination or sect) believe firmly not only in the Constitutional guarantee of separation of church and state, but also in the separation of church and art. To bring it down to specifics, no one on the editorial staff cares what religious belief a poet holds, what church he belongs to, what dogma he supports—he can be a Buddhist, a Jew, a Roman Catholic, a Jehovah's Witness, a Methodist, a Holy Roller, or whatever he chooses—and if he writes a *successful poem* out of his context as a thinking-feeling human being, he may appear on the Poetry Page. Furthermore—and this is just as important—he may hold no orthodox beliefs at all—he may be an agnostic or an atheist, a humanist or an existentialist—all of which rights are guaranteed him under the Constitution and fought for by our founding fathers whom you were quoting—and if he writes a successful poem out of *that* context he may also be accepted.

If one reacts to art as one would to someone who was with evangelical fervor trying to influence one's own religious beliefs— which, heaven knows, art does not try to do (this poem of Miss Flanner's, least of all)—then one is going to be offended every day in the week. This country is made up of a multitude of different beliefs—not one—and it is part of our tradition that we give freedom to all, whether or not we personally subscribe to them.

75

Miss Flanner happens to be a devout Quaker—but that is not the point. She could be a Druid for all we care. The important thing is that she is one of America's finest poets, and has written, in our opinion (which is the only opinion we have), a hauntingly beautiful and poignant expression of our modern dilemma. We are sorry you are offended, but we cannot with any integrity apologize for our choice.

I could not resist sending a copy of my reply to the editor-in-chief (who wrote back, "Wonderful!") and copies of both letters to Hildegarde Flanner, who was properly tickled, if amazed, by the whole thing:

It is bewildering, but on the whole pleasing, to hear that I am considered blasphemous by your New England reader. At least I am not dull. If anything is left of her, including the red-white-and-blue roundabouts that hold her together, after your excellent statement of values, so properly and clearly designed to scorch, it can only be because self-righteousness is more righteous than God himself.

Thank you, with all my heart, for your defense of me, both spirit and word, and let me say, I am proud to have been, even remotely, the cause of so fine a page on the subject of the relationship between conscience and writing. After all, the real meanings do lie in conscience, whatever the woe. The lucid indignation with which you wrote gave such a clear and crackling form to your response, a red-hot, smoking telegram, really. (One would like to think it got her up in the middle of the night and that she tripped over the cat in the dark.)

Your letter and the essay on values will always be precious to me—you cannot doubt how much I cherish them.

So if you want to get a response out of a poetry editor, just wave the flag or thump the Bible. We leap to the typewriter—and we probably always will. No one values his freedom more than the artist, even if he starves for it.

Chapter 8: Regional Poetry—East and West

ONE MIGHT SUPPOSE that a regional magazine like *Yankee* would feature regional poetry. It does not. As Poetry Editor I am frequently asked what my stand is on this sensitive point.

The first reason we do not—and probably the best—is that the majority of so-called regional verse submitted to my department is mighty miserable stuff.

Most people seem to think if they just stick to stone walls, birch trees, widows' walks and the good old sea, they have created poetry a New England magazine will find impossible to resist. Once in a while such subject matter is handled so skillfully that it is accepted at once. But this is the exception. Nothing so tempts a would-be poet to banality as "local color," unless it is love.

I was discussing this lamentable state of affairs with Hanson Kellogg, a poet born and brought up in Boston, son of a physician who also taught at Harvard, and a few of whose nostalgic regional pieces I have published. We came up with a few interesting conclusions.

First of all, a poet, when being a regionalist, deals with the landscape surrounding him, not merely to describe it, but to justify its importance, to say: "My environment is so good and so representative of everything beyond it that I need nothing else."

(No poet, however wide you extend the definition, was ever only a regionalist.)

This credo worked beautifully as long as it had to stand up against nothing more alien to it than its reverse—the romantic landscape made esoteric by distance in time or space. The perfect antithesis of lines like

> Behold her, single in the field,
> Yon solitary Highland lass!

as opposed to

> In Xanadu did Kubla Khan
> A stately pleasure-dome decree:

was pointed up by Wordsworth and Coleridge when they published *Lyrical Ballads* jointly.

But then poetry in English suffered a sea-change. The *interior* landscape provided the third side to a new eternal triangle. Until well into the nineteenth century poetry dealt with what is now the material of prose and made it memorable: Paul Revere's ride, for example. And it sold like *Peyton Place*, incredible as that now seems. Byron didn't wake one morning to find himself only famous. He found himself rich.

The reason is not hard to come by. Novels gained acceptance very slowly among the classes affluent enough to acquire literacy and a library. The Puritans damned them to hellfire as brain-rotting frivolities; the Cavaliers froze them with scorn as vulgarities. But poetry could be moral, didactic, lascivious, and elegant.

Scott and Dickens really made the first complete breakthrough of this barrier. Thereafter, poetry's field narrowed sharply, with the short, subjective lyric the favored form. As an art grows economically unrewarding, it tends to turn in on itself. (Note the decay of representative painting since the perfection of photography.)

There really has been little *pure* regional poetry since World War I. Radio, airplanes, everything else that shrinks the world, have had less to do with it than the consolidation of the newspaper chains, started, more or less, by Hearst, around the turn of the century. The rapid growth of AP and UP, too, and the development of boiler plate have contributed to the decline.

Boiler plate, so called because when curved onto a cylindrical press it resembles the sheet iron riveted onto old locomotives or water tanks, is a papier-mâché stereotype plate that prints a whole page of timely, because timeless, fillers and articles. Distributed in both Republican and Democratic flavors, it provided a cheap answer to the county paper's dearth of local news. It offered bulk and entertainment; more important it left the editor with only the outside four pages to fill, with the personals that held subscribers, and the legal notices that paid the bills. By standardizing everything else, it killed off local talent.

Before then newspapers were very much a do-it-yourself project. Even after the railroad, but prior to the Model T, people were regionalists. And their newspapers published their verse, though most of it was unspeakable. Some, however, when its authors had not read too many Victorians, was quite representative of a place in time. Most towns even had a semiprofessional eulogy writer who dressed up the obituary columns with rhymed epitaphs, for a price. A few of the best of these minor poets managed to make the magazines, but they had to drop the metrical private joke to do it.

Although the Far West produced many balladeers (best represented by Robert Service), it brought forth few good regional poets. The West Coast was in too great a state of flux at that time, was changing too fast, with too much Spanish history never correctly assimilated by "American" poets.

Consider Bret Harte as exemplar of all that was wrong with western regional verse. He came from the state of New York as a compositor at the wrong end of the '49 Gold Rush. He wrote such things as:

> You see this 'yer Dow
> Had the worst kind of luck;
> He slipped up somehow
> On each thing thet he struck.

Paradoxically enough, these poets are negligible because they were so little regionalists. If they weren't grinding out vaudeville monologues on gamblers and placer miners, they were translating Horace to demonstrate erudition. They did as poorly by the transients as they did by the Romans.

A notable exception must be made of Helen Hunt Jackson, the Amherst-born author of that minor *Uncle Tom's Cabin* for the Indians, *Ramona*. But even she is tainted by neoclassicism. Her excellent regional sonnet "Poppies Among the Wheat" deals with the east coast, not of the Pacific, as it might well have done, but of Italy on the Adriatic.

Meanwhile, back in Boston, things were not much better —at least in certain quarters. Take Lowell's second stanza of "The Courtin' " in which he slathered on dialect like a child with a pound of margarine:

> Zekle crep' up quite unbeknown
> An' peeked in thru the winder,
> An' there sat Huldy all alone,
> 'Ith no one nigh to hender.

Wasn't there any *good* regional verse on either shore?

Little on the West coast until Jeffers, and his was "impure" (going back to our original definition) and incidental to the great body of his work. As for Oliver Wendell Holmes, the true regionalist of New England, he lived in a microcosm he was able to exploit fully. During much of the nineteenth century, which he almost spanned, he had Boston in his pocket. And while it may not have been the Hub of the Universe, as advertised, it had certainly become the center of a Renaissance city state extending from Concord through Walden Pond to Salem and even west to Pittsfield when Melville was there.

Holmes so loved the town, and was so loved by it in return, that he seems tremendously evocative to many New Englanders.

Aside from Whitman, New York could boast of no individual to compare with Emerson, Thoreau, Longfellow, Whittier, Hawthorne, and the rest.

The South—to adopt for the moment a hint of its own florid style—dripped with the melancholy flamboyance of debased romanticism: a verbal Spanish moss infested with the redbugs of slavery and less systematic violences. And what fiery Virginian best exemplified all the power and excess of that macabre tradition before the Civil War? None other than Poe, a man born in Boston and obviously proud of it, since his first published title was *Tamerlane and Other Poems by a Bostonian*.

"Holmes's 'The Last Leaf'—incidentally it commemorates a Melville ancestor—brings back Boston to me," says Hanson Kellogg, "without a word of scenery, whereas Frost's 'Bending Birches' is chockful of scenery, but no more evokes rural New England than it does rural Wisconsin. I don't mean Frost isn't a good poet. He is. But he is *universal* in a sense that Holmes at his best was not."

If *Yankee* is to include regional verse, it had better be as good as, if not *like*, Holmes.

But perhaps we are asking too much. Even a few original birches would be welcome.

Part III: *As Teacher*

Chapter 9: *An Experiment in Creativity*

WHEN I WAS ASKED by a local college to teach an evening
poetry workshop in adult education I was faced with a
major doubt, not to mention several minor ones: Could this
most difficult of arts be taught at all? *Versification* could, of
course, be taught, but this did not interest me. Courses in
"Verse for Publication" or similar titles had already bloomed
and died for lack of support. Neither a university education
nor twenty years of writing had ever exposed me to a poetry

workshop or a class in "creative writing." Few professional writers of my acquaintance of either prose or poetry had ever attended such a class. They had learned, as had I, through the lonely, often agonizing effort of self-teaching and experiment.

And yet I was tempted and challenged by the request. In the course of reviewing hundreds of poems each month for *Yankee*, I had seen many a promising, but not yet successful, poem through painstaking revisions and had experienced with the poet the indescribable thrill of satisfaction when it finally came off. For other poet friends I had served on numerous occasions as literary midwife. The rewards were almost as great as those of actual creation. Perhaps something could be—not taught—but released. I decided to give it a try. Creativity could not be given to anyone, but it could be fostered. One could at least put reflector lights around even a small gleam.

The first thing I did was to inquire of other teachers of poetry what helpful ideas they might have for one as inexperienced as I. All of them emphasized *technique*. "They've got to learn the *craft*. Drill them on *forms*." I listened respectfully but in the end decided to do just the opposite. Oriented as I was in psychology and philosophy, it was simply not my way. I knew full well that if *I* were put into a class where the rhyme scheme of the villanelle or the metrics of the ballad were made of primary importance, I would never be able to write a line. With naive courage I decided to trust that knowledge. (Later, Hildegarde Flanner quoted Witter Bynner's advice to his class: "Get a book on forms if you want to —of course it won't do you a damn bit of good!" And I felt better.)

What then was primary? It seemed to me that before anyone could learn to write poetry, he must first know how to tap his own creative source. He must learn how to reach his own unconscious.

The second—and equally important—part of the job was, of course, to develop the raw material once it was brought to light. This transfer from feeling to thinking must

83

not be done solely on the basis of *form*. Form (in its narrower sense) was only one of the many aspects to be taken into consideration. Even more important were imagery, cadence, tone, the complexities of language, sound. To establish standards of taste in this regard, constant exposure to the best that had been written, especially of contemporary poetry, must be provided. We would *experience* poetry as well as study it.

In the third place, I believed strongly that this course could not be taught as an isolated art form. Poetry was not cut off from life. It *was* life. Music, painting, sculpture— above all, certain articles on the human predicament, even short stories, plays and novels—could illuminate the whole field and must not be disregarded.

With these three tenets clarified in my mind, I spent the next four months putting together eighteen class programs for the coming fall semester. The results were these: The two-and-a-half hour session was divided roughly in half, with a ten-minute break in the middle. I began each class with an "aperitif." Sometimes it was music—a Mozart sonata played on the Siena pianoforte, or Trappist monks singing Gregorian chants, or the lusty medieval songs of "Carmina Burana." Other times it was an excerpt from one of my favorite books: Thurber's *Fables*; James Agee's lyrical and tender *A Death in the Family*; *The Little Prince* of Saint-Exupéry; Rilke's *Letters to a Young Poet*. Once I spent ten minutes telling the group about my encounter with a poet from Ghana. We listened to Alan Watts tell a Chinese parable (on tape). We followed James Joyce's lilting Irish voice through the intricacies of "Anna Livia Plurabelle," and were spellbound by Howard Thurman reading the 139th Psalm as he had recorded it in my home.

This "aperitif" (fulfilling tenet No. 3) proved to be one of the happier features of the class. It served several purposes beyond the obvious one of exposing the group to other kinds of excellence. It provided a bridge from the busy-ness of their daily world to the more meditative and timeless world of art. It changed keys for us. Or, as one member put it, it was "the decorator's beautiful screen to close out the work area."

For the next forty or fifty minutes I talked informally about the problems of creativity and craftsmanship as they applied to poetry. These were carefully organized according to a sequence based as much on psychology as on literature. And it is here, I am told, that the structure of this class differed radically from others. I have no way of knowing whether this is true or not. I presented the material as I would have wanted it presented to me. The results were sometimes startling.

After an introductory lecture on "The Nature of Poetry" (the difference between poetry and prose, poetry and verse) and a ramble through comments by Wallace Stevens, T. S. Eliot, Emily Dickinson, A. E. Housman, Ezra Pound, Marianne Moore, and many others, I bravely launched into a brief but thorough discussion of "The Unconscious." My point of view was Jungian rather than Freudian, and I remember writing on the blackboard that first semester the quotation from *Modern Man in Search of a Soul*: "Any reaction to stimulus may be causally explained but the creative act, which is the absolute antithesis of mere reaction, will for ever elude the human understanding." In an hour I tried to cover for this attentive if slightly bewildered audience of fifty (I had asked for a maximum of twenty-five and twice that many had turned out) Jung's ideas of dreams, symbols, fantasies, and myth as they related to writing poetry. Basic to all these were his theories of the collective unconscious and archetypal images. "Whatever the structure of the unconscious may be, one thing is certain: it contains an indefinite number of motifs or patterns of an archaic character, in principle identical with the root ideas of mythology and similar thought forms." We talked about the fact that the poet had made great use of this theory, that the collective unconscious meant for him a storehouse of common experiences to which he could go. The inner world, if he could just reach it, had images and symbols which linked all men together regardless of national or racial origin.

85

What were some of the commonest archetypal images? We discussed them: house, sea, rock, angel, goddess, tree, devil, serpent, hero, horses, sun, fire, etc. Later on, these were brought up again and again, not only in the class poems, but in the examples of contemporary poetry read aloud (Dylan Thomas' "Fern Hill," for instance). For many in the class these were initially new (and sometimes irritating) concepts; later they proved stimulating and productive to an unusual degree.

With this orientation I asked the class to undertake an experiment. If it was true that we wrote out of our unconscious, how did we tap this mysterious well? Dorothea Brande had devised a method for *prose*.* I myself had followed it faithfully for a month several years before and knew its worth for *poetry*. In fact, I believed it held more value for the writing of poetry than anything else. One had to have this initial impulse or no amount of "fashioning" later would be of any use. Brande believed (and so did I) that the writer was half artist and half artisan—a split personality. The artist was emotional and childlike; the artisan was critical, discriminating. The difficult task was to get both sides of his nature into an integrated team. The first step was to split them farther apart. Brande's way was early morning, before-breakfast writing. I told my students:

> While you are still only half-awake (and your intellect temporarily in a state of torpor), reach for a pencil and paper and write. Have no thought of content, only of quantity. Write for a stated length of time, say, twenty minutes or half an hour. Put the material away and do not refer to it. The next morning try to increase your output. If you wrote a page the first morning, try to write two pages the second, and three the next. If you can't think of anything to write, describe in detail your frustration. Write down your dreams of the night before, or your plans for the day ahead. Write anything you like, uncritically. No one is going to read it but you. At the end of the week (and only then) gather up the material and read it.

What I promised them—and what they discovered for

*See *Becoming a Writer* by Dorothea Brande: Harcourt, Brace, 1934.

86

themselves—was, first of all, astonishing self-revelation. One sees one's own naked face, and while "know thyself" has always seemed to me basic to art as well as to religion, it is often a harrowing experience. But as the *Tao Te Ching* said, "He who knows others is wise. He who knows himself is enlightened."

At the next session each member told what the week's experiment had meant. For some it had proved immediately rewarding. Not only had they discovered new things about themselves, but they had uncovered dozens of ideas for poems.

For others the experiment had lasted only two or three mornings. It had proved too disturbing to continue, and yet, they admitted, it had not been time wasted. (Two years later one of this group brought me a poem she had just written out of this early morning material. She had not been able to use it then, but two years later it flowered.)

For still others, the whole idea was too antithetical to their previous conditioning to be helpful. I remember one woman angrily asserting that there was no such thing as the unconscious, that "all consciousness is one," and she could not be bothered with all this nonsense. She stomped out, never to return, not only hostile, but obviously frightened.

In large measure, however, this proved to be the single most constructive idea of the semester. It proved in a literary sense what psychologists have known a long time: that the unconscious is both archaic and new; that it rebels against the secondhand and the stereotyped. We all share archetypal images, but we have our own individual life experiences as well. It is, of course, the derivative, the cliché that every teacher of poetry fights. The point was made early and forcibly.

Along with discussions of "levels of inspiration," "what kind of person writes poetry," the "disability theory of art" (is an artist *sicker* than his fellow man?), and "should a poet live in the world or apart from it?" the students began to work over the raw material brought up out of the murky seas of their own depths. First, they brought to class whatever "seeds" of ideas or feelings might possibly grow into poems. Sometimes it was a complete line, sometimes just a phrase, but one which brought with it the rhythm, the language, the *direction* of the poem. This was the *donnée* without which there could be no poem and which one must learn, not only to recognize, but to trust.

Then followed lectures on:

The Play Impulse in Writing Poetry. Poetry is not *just* an intellectual game, but it is that too.

The Poet as Artisan. Every poem brings its own form, its own architecture.

Imagery and Metaphor. At one of three lectures on this subject I brought in a piece of jade found on a California beach and passed it around the class, not only to see, but also to feel. The next week they brought in lists of images relative to the stone and its origins; the following week they brought their poems. Some were extraordinary. This exercise also served to show how effective *concrete* subject matter could be.

Symbolism.

Language. Let's get rid of Victorian potted rubber plants; the revolution in poetry in the French symbolists, in Pound and Eliot; concrete images vs. abstract statements; the great difference between simplicity and banality.

The Dramatic Structure in Poetry. Precision in poetry; verbs and nouns more important than adjectives and adverbs.

Rhythm and Melody in Poetry. The wrong rhythm in a poem is like trying to write a Mass to a polka; the pace of a poem; something about metrics. (It is interesting to note that in planning this course I waited until the twelfth lecture before enlightening them on iambs, trochees, pentameter, dactyl, or caesura. By this time they were not afraid of them.)

Rhyme, the Discipline and Difficulties of Free Verse, etc.

Why Poems Fail. The failure of insight, attitude; the mat–

ter of imitation vs. influence; the difference between "self-expression" and poetry.

How to Revise. "It is not inspiration that exhausts one," said Yeats, "it is art."

The Audience. Whom do we write for? Study of markets, with exhibits of about seventy-five magazines, and a listing dividing them into "Top Drawer," "Excellent," "Good," "Fair to Middling," and "Ugh."

Against this background, the students learned what it means to *fashion* a poem; that art is not only born but *made*. They learned, sometimes painfully, that a poem is not an essay on life, but the re-creation of an experience. The "pains of turning blood into ink," to quote Mr. Eliot, were never minimized.

My sources for these informal talks were many. First of all I drew on John Ciardi's excellent book *How Does a Poem Mean?* (Houghton Mifflin, 1959) and Elizabeth Drew's equally fine *Poetry, a Modern Guide to Its Understanding and Enjoyment* (Dell Publishing Co., 1959). Supplementing these I have a bibliography of some forty-six assorted books and articles I had collected over the years, plus the accumulation of a four-drawer file full of related material—everything from Zen to semantics to political economics to natural science to porcelains of the T'ang Dynasty—on which I frequently drew. My own experiences as a poet and editor were, of course, very helpful.

The second half of the session was sometimes a literary and critical free-for-all. As long as they didn't all talk at once, I never interfered with expressions of opinion. The climate was, at the least, relaxed and easy. As many poems as possible were put on the blackboard. I read each poem aloud to give it the best presentation possible. No poem was ever submitted for class criticism that did not have *some* merit. Because of the size of the class, each member was allowed to hand in one poem a week, plus as many revisions as he liked. I gave back written critiques on each poem (as detailed as possible; always honest). If the poem was revisable, I put a small R beside it. I kept the actual poem in the member's folder, along with a carbon copy of my critique. In this way I was always able to relate what a student had done to what he had previously accomplished, to his own literary handicap. This proved to be a very practical idea. At the end of the semester I handed back the whole file. I urged each student to keep working papers on every poem he wrote, and it was always one of the high spots of an evening when I could share with the class the various stages of a poem—from mediocre beginning to triumphant final form. These sessions of hard, concentrated, often exhausting application of whatever they had learned from the lectures brought into sharp focus the points I had tried to make. The arguments were often heated. There were also many laughs. The teacher's job was not only to referee, but to hold her ground without emotion when she felt she was right. In other words, high standards, but no rigidity. One learns early how to dismiss gently the inept comment or how to translate for a group of such widely different backgrounds an intellectually abstract statement from one of the better read students. As one of them remarked, "The only common denominator of this group is respect for each other's work—and it is all we need!"

They went a long way too toward learning one of the most important things in any art: how to separate one*self* from one's work. At first, criticism of a poem tended also to be taken as a personal attack. Gradually they were able to put distance between themselves and the poems, and with the new detachment came greater freedom to use their skills.

Each session closed with the reading of some example of good contemporary poetry, to send them away with the best ringing in their ears. During the course of a year we managed to cover a range that included Emily Dickinson, Stephen Crane, Isabella Gardner, Abbe Huston Evans, Richard Wilbur, Howard Nemerov, Robert Lowell, Theodore Roethke, Karl Shapiro, W. S. Merwin, James Dickey, and many, many others. Dylan Thomas and T. S. Eliot spoke to us on records; and others, like Kenneth Rexroth, Eric Barker, and John Crowe Ransom, read by means of the anthology tape I had made over a period of years.

Incidentally, I never read from my own work. Some teachers, I know, use this type of class as a platform for trying out their own poems. In my opinion, this is a mistake for many reasons, chief among which is the danger of putting before the class an image of how you personally have dealt with poetry, thus inviting imitation. I was rewarded when one member exclaimed, "Now I know why this class is so wonderful. You don't teach us to write like *you*; you teach us to write like ourselves!"

The "proof of the pudding" was, first of all, literary. Did the students actually write better at the end of the year than they did when they began? The question has been asked of me often. The answer, of course, is that some did and some did not. The method did not take with everyone. I can truthfully say, however, that the percentage of improvement was high, and some of it striking. At the end of the year we made a tape recording of the best poem of each student. It is a highly creditable, if uneven, anthology, even by my critical standards. Many of them had started out feebly but had ended successfully. These were the real triumphs. I remember in particular a man who worked as a janitor in a large office building. His first submissions were incredibly bad, exhibiting every fault of content and form. They were sentimental effusions of the birdie-with-the-yellow-bill school. Of all the students in the class I would have placed him at the bottom of the list. His enthusiasm, however, remained undimmed through weeks of blunt but patient criticism. Suddenly one evening he turned in a poem that was fresh, imaginative, controlled. I could hardly believe my eyes. "What happened to you?" I asked in astonishment. He twinkled at me, then whispered, "*You* happened to me."

Another member, a girl who taught physiotherapy by day, had been fond of turning in a kind of beatnik verse, full of far-out imagery and eccentric structure. After weeks of this kind of experimentation that communicated almost nothing but her own confusion, she submitted a poem that rang with original simplicity. The class cheered. A man who had written nothing but immature imitations of "Howl" finally turned to his own rich background and wrote a moving but unsentimental evocation of his Jewish mother. "You taught me how to stop shouting," he admitted later.

While no emphasis was placed on marketing, several members did sell poems during that year to such publications as *The Atlantic*, *The Christian Science Monitor*, *The Galley-Sail*, *Coastlines*, *Voices*, and *The Georgia Quarterly Review*.

The other proofs were nonliterary—and surprising. The ramifications of this kind of experiment in creativity penetrated into many other areas than poetry. The early-morning writing was, I am sure, responsible for some of this, but not all. In my effort to keep the field as wide as possible, I inadvertently unlocked more doors than I had anticipated. ("Have you ever thought of taking up group therapy?" one of the students asked with a grin.) At the end of the first semester each member wrote out his critical evaluation of the class, and the reports (many of them unsigned) were both candid and moving:

"I've lost my intellectual snobbishness."

"I'm not nearly so shy."

"This class stretched my mind in dozens of ways, and I never dreamed it had that much elasticity."

"I'm still not ready to call the world a friend, but now I can admit that she does smile once in a while . . . and it is a lovely sight."

"You won't belive it, but even my relationship to my daughter is better!"

"Now I have everything. . . ."

Perhaps May Sarton was right when she said teaching was also "the care of souls." The teacher's role is also that most difficult one of all—that of catalyst. As one of the class remarked, "It's not just you, Mrs. Burden, it's the *class!*"

Chapter 10: Second and Third Semesters

LUCKILY, only about half the original group stayed on for the second semester. No one new was allowed in, though several applied. One young thing, frustrated at my refusal to let her join, protested, "But I've written over seven hundred poems—on *all* subjects!"

I had prepared the lectures for the first semester during the previous summer. I was free, therefore, during the unwinding of the first eighteen weeks to feel my way into a second term. I was still unwilling to devote it to form. That could come in Part Three (and did). It seemed to me that a little more depth was needed for those who had the determination and the talent to stay on. It was time to go not only forward but *down*. This meant greater student participation in what had formerly been the lecture half of each session.

I remember saying on the opening night (what in fact I had been saying all along) that I had always been of the opinion that poetry did not belong on a peninsula from life and that, therefore, it could not be studied in this manner, in terms solely of aesthetics, or of technique, forms, etc., in terms only of itself.

"When one studies any art deeply enough, one is quickened at a center which includes everything," I said. "By life in its totality. That is why I thought we would explore the large areas of the human predicament—not, of course, as such, but as they relate to us through our art form which is poetry. And within these abstractions we will search for our own specifics. In other words, we will try to write about them."

Taking guidance from Elizabeth Drew's *Poetry, a Modern Guide to Its Understanding and Enjoyment* (but modifying them to suit their own preferences), the class chose for its discussion topics:

Time
Nature (including animals)
Love
Social comment
Loneliness and the search for identity
Nostalgia
Religion
Death
Humor
Children's poetry
Haiku

Two other ingredients went into the broth of this second semester: guest stars chosen from the local community of professionals came every other week to give a talk or read from their own work; and twenty-to-thirty minute papers were prepared by each student on a poet of his own choosing.

Assignments were every other week in order to give time for more revisions—very important in an advanced class—and followed the topic of the period. I felt these were so broad that no student would feel cramped. It was not like being asked to write a poem on autumn merely because the calendar said October.

The "aperitifs" continued as before, ranging widely from Jamaican folk songs to arias sung by Elizabeth Schwarzkopf, from Peter De Vries' short stories to a recording of T. S. Eliot reading from *Four Quartets*, to a photographic exhibit by a leading modern artist—anything, in short, that I particularly loved in the arts. Shared enthusiasm has always seemed to me one of the most valuable products of a good teacher. It is contagious. So many of my students later told me that they had gone out afterward and bought the books or the records from which the aperitifs had been drawn and then had given copies away as gifts to friends.

The second half of each session was, as before, devoted to a discussion of poems by members of the class, with selections put on the board and a loose, though controlled, powwow resulting. The steam of these encounters between the sensitive, though talented, amateur and an intelligent, though amateur, group of critics, presided over by a teacher who was herself a poet, was often enough to blur the windows, to say nothing of occasionally threatening to lift the roof. Once I had them all exchange poems and write critiques of each other's work, anonymously if they preferred.

The groans of the students the next week when they described the agonies they had gone through to write an honest piece of criticism were appreciated by all of us, especially me.

The written critique was something I had begun the first semester and continued during the second. It was a demanding, and sometimes exhausting, discipline for me, but I felt it was essential for the student who was learning how

95

to revise, and almost as important for me inasmuch as I continued to keep carbon copies of these critiques with the poems in individual folders, returning the critiques each week, but handing back the poems only at the end of the semester. In this way I kept track of individual progress, or lack of it, as I could not possibly have done otherwise.

I also laid greater emphasis this semester on markets, advising students specifically where to send poems I considered ready for submission. And I urged them to bring in new magazines they found on the large newsstands they had learned to frequent. In that way we all benefited from examining close at hand the various verse magazines and quarterlies of the day—some excellent, some dreadful, some enduring, others ephemeral, but all interesting and providing a good view of the wide range of published poetry in America today. I was also glad to note that without prodding one member of the class observed, "It looks to me as though as much *bad* poetry is being published today as good."

The visiting "stars" were drawn from my personal acquaintance. The Los Angeles area is home to a large group of professional poets. Others are here on fellowships or for lectures. That year we were privileged to hear: Jennette Yeatman, poet and teacher of modern poetry at the Pasadena College of Liberal Arts; Margaret Widdemer, poet and novelist from New York; Susana Mueller, renowned Chilean painter, who brought an exciting exhibit of children's art from her own students; Hildegarde Flanner, the well-known California poet; Raymond Holden, New England poet, out in Los Angeles for the winter; Gene Frumkin, then editor of *Coastlines*, and a poet; Mrs. Edward Weismiller, who writes under the name of Ames Rowe Quentin and who substituted charmingly for her husband.

To illustrate the hour devoted to poetry *for* and *by* children, I surprised the class by bringing in the eight-year-old daughter of a friend, whose precociousness in reading poetry had long delighted everyone who knew her. My introduction of "Miss Martha Pyne" as "leading authority on the art of writing for children" was followed by the door opening and pint-sized Miss Pyne, in pinafore, entering. She sat on the desk facing the class, her short legs dangling over the edge, and gave a poised reading of her own favorites.

Another out-of-the-ordinary evening was the one I planned to examine the influence of the Oriental on modern poetry. The aperitif that night was Japanese *koto* music. This was followed by one side of Alan Watts's fine record on haiku—his essay on the subject. Then I showed examples of *sumi* ink drawings from an out-of-print book I have always treasured, *Artistry in Ink*. I remember how my enthusiasm for Muchi's *Persimmons* baffled some of the class. A few years later I received a letter from a member of that class, saying that at last she had been able to see what *I* had seen in that exquisite work and that she was so grateful to the class for having introduced her to it.

Then I played the other side of Alan's record where, accompanied by ancient instruments, he and a Japanese girl read haiku, first in Japanese, then in English. Several of the class were already writing haiku and tanka, but for all of us this more careful explication of the pared-down, suggestive quality of poetry (and other related art forms) was illuminating and provocative.

For those who are interested in the actual construction of the two-and-one-half-hour class sessions for use in their own teaching, and bewildered perhaps by the recital of so many ingredients, let me be more explicit. There were basically two different kinds of program, and they alternated. For instance, the session on Time went like this, with the 150 minutes divided as follows:

10 min. Aperitif: Story of "Versailles Adventure" in *Unbidden Guests* by William Oliver Stevens—an authenticated ghost story showing dislocation of time as we know it.

30 min. Paper by class member on Conrad Aiken.

45 min. Discussion of time, with students sitting in a circle,

97

all contributing, monitored by me. Some of the concepts discussed:

1. Fleeting time:
   "O world! O life! O time!..."—Shelley
   "When I consider everything that grows..."—Shakespeare
   "Gather ye rosebuds while ye may..."—Herrick
2. Old age: "Little Gidding"
3. Dunne's *An Experiment with Time*—relationship of dreams to time.
4. Difference between time and space. Time is not just another dimension of space.
5. Eternity vs. endless time.
6. The Oriental idea of time.
7. The difference between clock time and psychological time.
8. Time as a measure of motion. (I asked the class to close their eyes and think of themselves as living on through time, moving continuously from the past into the future. How fast were they going? Sailing with a slow wind, or going by jet? How slow a sensation of time can they get? Change from jet propulsion to sail. Then change from sail to snail. The hour hand of a clock? How slow can slow be?)
9. The eternal Now.

10 min. Break.

50 min. Discussion of class poems.

5 min. Reading aloud of some poems on time—Andrew Marvell, Dylan Thomas, Eric Barker.
Assign poems on time (good for two weeks).

The seminars gave a context in which I was able to introduce selections from the writings of a wide variety of people: Thurber, E. B. White, Camus, Oppenheimer, Simone Weil, Meister Eckhardt, Charles Morgan, Jung, Sugrue, Erich Fromm, to mention only a few. One of the more interesting tapes I played was Norman Cousins' story of his first visit to Albert Schweitzer's hospital—part of a lecture I had heard at Occidental College.

The next week illustrates the alternative program:

10 min. Aperitif: recording of T. S. Eliot's "Burnt Norton" from *Four Quartets*.

30 min. Paper by class member on Rilke.

45 min. Talk by Mrs. Yeatman on the physics of sound as related to the language of poetry.

10 min. Break.

50 min. Discussion of class poems.

5 min. Reading aloud of more poems on time.

Two excursions outside of class proved rewarding. One was to visit Susana Mueller's home and studio, not only to see more of her fascinating collection of children's paintings, but to discuss at greater length than the class period had allowed her philosophy of teaching, her ideas of evoking the creative self—quite similar to my own ideas, but evoked by other means. The importance of the child-self in all art was not lost on the class.

The second outing was a trip to Ojai one Saturday to hear the Indian teacher Krishnamurti speak in the famous oak grove. His name had come up several times in our seminar discussions, drawn there, I admit, by my own enthusiasm for the man and his ideas. When I announced one evening that he would be giving a series of talks and that I was going up for the first one, several members asked whether they could go too. More than a dozen of us drove the 125 miles, picnicking on the way. The encounter with this remarkable man, surely one of the most original and pure-spirited of modern philosophers, was something none of us would forget.

Just a word about the third semester. For the sake of

those who may be planning a similar class, let me say it was devoted to studying traditional forms and meters in the belief that the students were now ready for this kind of discipline, that it was important for them to get inside tradition rather than to stand shivering outside of it. I asserted that it would reinforce and strengthen their own styles and might, indeed, release them into new creativity. Sometimes, I said, an increase in obstacle and limitation forces creativity into a narrower corner and thus increases *heat*.

Their texts were Robert Hillyer's *First Principles of Verse* and Babette Deutsch's *Poetry Handbook*.

I opened the semester by a lecture on prosody. From then on the class took over more of the program than had heretofore been practical. The schedule went like this:

Every two weeks a different poetic form was taken as the subject. The class was divided into pairs, with one pair assigned to each form. One member of the pair did the major research; the "assistant," or "alternate," looked up the examples, selections to be read aloud, interesting tapes or records to enrich the topic under discussion, the aperitif. Every other meeting I officiated as critic over the attempts of the class to write in the form under consideration. These were the ballad, the ballade, the sonnet, minor French forms such as the triolet, rondel, and rondeau, the villanelle, the sestina, and Japanese forms such as haiku and tanka, and the cinquain (influenced by the Oriental).

It goes without saying that I learned as much as I taught during those years. Aside from the extensive research I was forced to do into the art of poetry and into exactly what I thought about it, I learned to my own satisfaction that adults will work and work hard if they can see some progress in their skills and some self-revelation. I learned what a hunger there is for more meaning in their lives. We covered a lot of ground together—psychology, philosophy, education, religion, music, the whole field of aesthetics. I proved to myself my original idea of what a poetry workshop should and could be—that you can't teach poetry unless you teach a great deal *more* than poetry.

Epilogue: *A Way of Knowing*

EVERY POET who ever lived has probably been asked at least
once—and you may be sure it was by a nonpoet—why he
writes poetry. Auden says he writes poetry "because it is
fun." (This is not as foolish a reply as it may seem.) Dame
Edith Sitwell once snarled in her well-bred way at such a
question by replying, "Been to the zoo lately? Go down and
ask the tiger why he wears his stripes!" Hildegarde Flanner
has said that one of the reasons she writes poetry is because

life is poignant and fleeting and she is seeking to preserve it in a poem against time and oblivion.

All of these answers seem to me to be valid: we write poetry because it is a sophisticated and subtle form of "play"; we also write because it is our stripe, our nature, because we cannot help it; and we write to arrest, even if briefly, the swift movement of our confusion and to make some order of it.

To all these reasons, however, I would add another—and for me this is by far the most important. We write poetry in order to *know*.

I remember that I was less than half as old as I am now when I first discovered this for myself. My father had been dying slowly for months; one day, crossing the busy intersection of State and Randolph in Chicago, I was seized by a line of poetry that later became the last line of the first poem I ever sold to *Poetry*: "And death is no less terrible because it is quiet." Almost blind with the incandescence of this idea I made my way to the other side of the street and walked back to the office repeating the line over and over to myself. I knew I had a *donnée*—that first magical beginning of a poem that always seems to be handed to one by an unseen hand around the corner of an invisible door. But what I realized *at the same time* was that until that moment I had not known that this was my attitude toward death! For me, then and now, this direct, stark encounter with inevitability without diminishing or prettifying it was part of my acceptance and enduring of it. Many years later I began another poem on death with the line, similar in concept, "The loss is absolute; do not be misled." But I ended it: "Death is death only for the living. / Listen—night will die with a young sound." Here I carry the insight a step further. And what I will emphasize again and again is that it was *the poem which led me*, not vice versa. In other words, I didn't have the idea and then find the words with which to clothe it. I found it in the poetry itself. The insight, if paraphrased out of the poem, into prose, would not be at all the same insight as in its original context.

If poetry is "a way of knowing," it is only fair to ask: a way of knowing *what?* The all-inclusive answer, of course, is: "A way of knowing *reality*." But this is a big, vague word.

Let us see if we can break it down a little.

First, it is a way of knowing the so-called objective world, the world of "things." No naturalist, for example, is any keener in observation than a poet. But the essential difference between the two is that while both are fascinated by the inner and outer nature of things, the naturalist will analyze his subject in terms of facts; the poet will see his subject in terms of analogy as well. Take the description of a bat: "Any of an order (Chiroptera) of placental mammals with fore-limbs modified to form wings. They are the only mammals capable of true flight." Now listen to what D. H. Lawrence wrote:

> A twitch, a twitter, an elastic shudder in flight
> And serrated wings against the sky,
> Like a glove, a black glove, thrown up at the light
> And falling back.

From *Collected Poems*: The Viking Press, New York, 1929.

Dylan Thomas described a Welsh village in winter as "a bandaged town." I know I shall never forget Marianne Moore's mussel shell "opening and shutting itself like an injured fan," nor the mouse's tail hanging out of the cat's mouth like a shoelace. To Howard Moss pine needles are "stiff as horsehair." Shakespeare describes bees as "the singing masons building roofs of gold," and Ciardi once painted a simple pear in these words:

>   The pear
> was the yellow of a glaze but sanded dull
> then lit again by my lamp. These first two lights
> were then burned red from below. And up through
> that, the black and umber of ripeness freckled it.
>
> And somewhere never placeable in that yellow
> a memory of green misted its presence.

From "Cezanne," in *As If*: Rutgers University Press, 1955. Used by permission of the author.

Nor is it only the natural world that fascinates a poet.
Marcia Masters (Edgar Lee Masters' daughter) remembers
the "Graveyard at Genoa" in these lines:

> The cold imaginings of stone
> Have dressed the dead more marvellously than life.
> Clusters of proud tableaux are robed in awe;
> Lace foamed of gloom, and granite silk
> Nourishing a sadness in each fold,
> And skirts of grandeur where grey violets lie untouched,
> Or crumble downward past the huge proclaiming
>   hands . . .

From *Intent on Earth*: The Candlelight Press, New York, 1965.

Richard Wilbur looked out of his Rome apartment at the
laundry hanging on the line and wrote "Outside the open
window / The morning air is all awash with angels."* And
Eric Barker, listening to the foghorns in San Francisco,
wrote:

> Across their shrouded pasture, through the night,
> The bass-voiced bulls are calling one another.
> They chew up bales of wet sea-wool like grass
> And bawl stupendous love no fog can smother.

From "Listen, the Fog Horns," in *Looking for Water*: October House, New
York, 1964. Used by permission of the author.

In each instance—and in many, many others—the poet
has added his own dimension to fact. And he has added it
for all of us—for all time.

To put it a little differently, the poet sees the world very
much as a child does—but with the mind of a seer. Or as one
of my class once said, "I think, Mrs. Burden, that you want
poets to observe like four-year-olds, but think like God!"
And she wasn't far wrong. Certainly it implies the need for
wonder, that most prized of attitudes. We must be able to
explore, but not exploit, our own astonishment.

What else is poetry capable of knowing?

It is a unique and sure way of knowing the subjective
world of feelings.

*From "Love Calls Us to the Things of This World," in *Things Of This
World*: Harcourt, Brace & World, New York, 1956.

Epilogue: A Way of Knowing

To a poet, subject is object—in a way a psychologist never even approximates. In other words, his own emotional world, vague, turbulent, confused as it always is, becomes the raw material out of which he creates order, meaning, and, sometimes, even a kind of realization. One has to move back from an emotion before one can write *about* it or *from* it. Or, as MacLeish once said, "The test of a poem is not its power to create emotion but to withstand emotion."* And not just pure emotion, but the mixed-up, ambivalent froth of feeling that is our usual state. Many times I have discovered in the writing of a poem terror side by side with welcome; aversion mixed up with attraction—and it is the poem that does the disentangling.

Parenthetically, I think one of the reasons why pure joy is less often a subject for poetry than its opposite is because joy needs no interpretation. It *is*. Which reminds me of how Dr. Howard Thurman, the famous Negro clergyman, describes his own feeling of pure contentment. He calls it "is-ing." "I just want to *is*," he'll say—and no further definition is necessary. Pain is something else again. We often need art to help us interpret pain. It is part of the unknown. Perhaps that is why so many poems about joy are clouded with other emotions—it seems to need that pinch of alloy to be tough enough to withstand itself.

This joy mingled with wistfulness is beautifully exemplified in Hildegarde Flanner's poem "Eve of Elegy," about a cicada:

> The last cicada prays for love
> This bright November night,
> Singing alone to his own song
> The quavering gospel of delight
> With which he late persuaded
> The delicate mob of pearly kin,
> The music-shaken mystics
> Who tremuloed to him.
> Sing on, you widowed melody,

*Quoted from "Notebooks" by Archibald MacLeish, *Poetry*, October 1948: copyright by the Modern Poetry Association. Used by permission of the editor of *Poetry* and the author.

Tender monotonist,
With sweet obsessed voice
   —Rejoice, rejoice—
A music that should mourn its dead,
(Where pathos dangles on the twig)
But stutters with hope and joy instead.
Sing on, so solitaire, so wed.

From *Yankee*, November 1960.

I am sure that before Miss Flanner had finished this poem she had discovered for herself, and luckily for us, that marvelous insight about pathos dangling on the twig and "music that should mourn its dead / But stutters with hope and joy instead." (How the precision of a poet's language does brighten our dark—that wonderful verb, "stutters," for a cicada.)

In my own memory I can sort out many similar instances of poetry somehow lighting up and therefore reconciling me to a feeling that threatened to overwhelm. "I shape a world to rest my anger on / Of all things hard and motionless," I wrote at twenty-two, at a time when frustration seemed to paralyze me, and I could not collaborate with the inevitable. And once, islanded by that isolation everyone is subject to at some time or other, I wrote a poem called "Absence" in which I likened that feeling to being suddenly surrounded by space, and where the image of the hawk is implied, but never stated. "I am clutched by absence as by a claw," I wrote, and suddenly it wasn't so terrible anymore.

Of course, no one ever wrote of the lonely agony of the soul more eloquently than Emily Dickinson:

After great pain a formal feeling comes—
The nerves sit ceremonious like tombs . . .

From *The Complete Poems of Emily Dickinson*, copyright 1929, 1957, by Mary L. Hampson. Used by permission of the publishers, Little, Brown and Company, Boston, Massachusetts.

Or of hope:

Hope is the thing with feathers
That perches in the soul . . .

Ibid.

A scholarly dissertation toward a Ph.D. in psychology could never hope to equal that for precision. Or profundity. It was Emily's insight, and Emily's honesty, and now it is also ours.

One of the demands that poetry makes upon us is that ancient dictum "know thyself." I tell my class, in the words of Theodore Roethke's kittycat bird, "Whoever you are, be sure it's you." Every poet learns—to his pain and astonishment—that no one else can breathe and burn for him. No one else can *see* for him. This is the artist's responsibility, and to shirk it is to fall into the terrible tedium of the stereotype, the cliché, the banal. It is, simply, to fail. What a poet turns his attention to is a reflection of himself. What he is aware of, what involves him most deeply, all this he translates into his art. All this, he *is*.

In brief, we have been saying that poetry is a special way of knowing the world and ourselves. Prose talks *about* experience; poetry re-creates it, both for the poet and the reader. Poetry illumines the relationship between the I and the not-I. And here we nudge the world of philosophy, the area of meanings, of values, of metaphysics. This is another level of knowledge, this is the tracking of that elusive bird with the long tail-feathers called Truth. And man (this tricky fusion of the finite and the infinite) has been hard at it since he first took up residence on this planet number 3. Yeats says that at about thirty "any writer who is anything of an artist comes to understand that all a work of art can do is show us the reality that is within our minds and the reality that our minds look on."* What else is there?

If it is true that poetry and philosophy wrestle with some of the same ideas, where do they differ? At its most profound, poetry is concerned with meaning, but not meaning confined to a theorem. A poet doesn't generalize very much. He believes that the finite and specific lead to reality; he travels to the universal by way of the concrete. The poetic imagination is always making judgments; it is constantly choosing between what is real and what is false, but it is doing so within the poem itself. Poetry persuades by meta-

*MacLeish, *op. cit.*

phor and suggestion instead of by syllogism, by symbol instead of by abstraction. Poets who have tried to turn into philosophers in the mistaken idea that whatever is true is also beautiful, and that whatever is beautiful is automatically a poem, have done the ancient lovely girl no good. A philosopher advances by logic; a poet leaps by image. Where he is now is no guarantee of where he will be an eye-wink from now. He has his own logic—the logic of connotation, not denotation. A poem gives off considerable steam, I have often said, not just because it is going somewhere, but from the heat of its associations.

What, then, about science? In the main, I think we can say that the scientist and the poet have little in common. The scientist proceeds to his kind of knowledge by analysis and formulation. ("Whatever can be *known*," says Bertrand Russell, "can be known by means of science.") Poets insist that poetry has no morals or messages to deliver, but that it is capable of a kind of knowledge that is beyond slide rules and test tubes—in other words, that truth is more marvelous than fact. Science is knowledge by abstraction; poetry is knowledge by synthesis.* Poetry presents the world inside and the world out there—through the marriage of inner and outer vision—not by translating them into generalizations or laws or averages, but by bringing us to confront them as they are: man and foghorn in direct encounter, as though seen for the first time; woman and cicada, face to face.

Nor do religion and art have much in common, though each is a positive search for truth. Religion usually runs the gamut all the way from declaring that the truth is unequivocally revealed by God through a particular theology to the position that Reality is of a Being or a category of existence which is inaccessible to man. The poet, the artist, affirms over and over that Reality can be known, but only in snatches. In holy snatches. And he is continually seeking

*See "Why Do We Teach Poetry?" by Archibald MacLeish, copyright © 1956, by The Atlantic Monthly Company, Boston, Massachusetts, 02116. By permission of *The Atlantic Monthly* and the author.

108

to confine these snatches in a frame, and then to let them go. He is not inclined to codify or to crystalize these moments of realization into system, into dogma. (And here I remember what Dr. Howard Thurman—he is very quotable!—said about dogma: "Dogma is the rationalization of someone *else's* personal religious experience.") A poet insists that each man be his own cosmologist, his own theologian, his own *experiencer*. One may believe, I think, in the power of man to experience truth, without labeling it Absolute Truth. This means ultimately that all art is involved in some degree with heresies.

As a matter of fact, a poet is more inclined to ask questions of Life than to assert conclusions. He has no mania for certainty. Is it so? he asks over and over. Is it really so? How? Why? And the poet is always rejecting the answers that the logical scientists and philosophers and theologians are eager to hand him.* The poet, I repeat, has his own answers.

Man has always been fascinated by incarnation. In poetry incarnation has a different meaning: *flesh becomes word*, if only for a moment.

> The poet's eye in a fine frenzy rolling,
> Doth glance from heaven to earth, from earth to heaven
> And as imagination bodies forth
> The forms of things unknown, the poet's pen
> Turns them to shapes and gives to airy nothing
> A local habitation and a name.
>
> *—A Midsummer Night's Dream*

Shakespeare brought to his poetry not just a lifetime, but all the time there was!

What then is left? The answer is art, and the meaning that art reveals. And poetry, in particular? Not meaning abstracted out of the poem, as we have said, but within the matrix of the poem. For in any art, the whole is always greater than the sum of its parts. In poetry the language is in the rhythms, and the rhythms are in the sounds, and the sounds are in the images, and everything is in everything

---

*For further discussion of this, see "Introduction" to *Four Poets on Poetry* by Don Cameron Allen, Johns Hopkins Press, 1959.

else, tugging against each other. The resultant is not just tension, but meaning. As Karl Shapiro pointed out,* because poetry uses language it is assumed that poetry functions as language. The same word used in a line of prose and a line of poetry is really two different words, not even similar, except in appearance. Everything a poet selects for his poem —its structure, its cadences, its metaphors—depends on everything that he is. His poem is organized both intuitively and consciously. Ask a poet exactly how he constructs a poem, and he would have a difficult time telling you. But one thing he knows: part of it is given him, and part he builds. As Valéry said, "God gives you the first line, but you have to work like hell for the second!" And from the second to the third and from the third to the fourth, the poem gives birth to itself. Art is never inspiration alone. It is artifice. It is vision—and revision. A poem may begin in a word, but it ends in something else because the poet has allowed it to build a context on the way—to build relationships. And it is these dancing relationships between words, and between meter and sound, and meaning and image— and between all of them together—that make the poem, that make the instrument of knowledge.†

Now to gather up these ideas and carry them just one step further. Poetry is not Mr. Keats's urn, full of beauty and truth. Poetry is a thrust into time, and against time. And it is one of the few actions left to us which can *create the thing it finds* (to quote MacLeish again). Poetry never really grows up, it has been said. I recall with pleasure a cartoon strip in the Los Angeles *Times* of a wise old man and a smug little boy with his nose in a book. Overhead is a dragon carrying a load of people on his back. The old man asks the little boy, "Ever see a dragon carrying people, son?" The little boy replies, without looking up from his book, "Dragons are a myth for untutored minds." ("Oh," says the old man.) "Even if they existed, they wouldn't fly." ("Ah," says the

*From "Prosody As the Meaning," by Karl Shapiro, *Poetry*, March 1949: copyright by the Modern Poetry Association. Used by permission of the editor.
†John Ciardi also discusses this in *How Does a Poem Mean?*: Houghton Mifflin, Boston, Massachusetts, 1960.

old man.) "And if they flew, they wouldn't carry people." "Eddication is a wonderful thing," says the wise old man, as the dragon flies out of sight. "It enables me to see things as they really are," says the little boy, still not looking up.

A poet does see things as they really are—including dragons. He is a revealer of secrets, an uncoverer of darkness, a skinner of surfaces. And because he sees the world as though it were the first dawn of creation, he participates in some degree in the creation. The poet can be a kind of god, producing a new world with each poem by the wand of his pen. All art, I think, is a refusal to consent to the world as a static condition, as it is. And yet, paradoxically, it comes through first accepting the world as it is, and then transfiguring it. It is a cheering thing in this day, when so much of our lives seems to be ordered, that in this area we are still free. Free to transform the commonplace into the enchanted, and the enchanted into the familiar. For by marshaling the little pieces of reality which the poet finds significant into a structure, into a poem, this is just what he does. Every experience uncovers a new aspect of truth; every bit of knowledge the poet acquires through his poem adds to the knowledge of the world.

As the poet moves through his poem, trying to understand what he knows, he is making a self as well as a poem. John Holmes, the New England poet, said that if you see three men walking down the street, all looking very much alike, and you wonder which one is the poet, go up and "twang them." The poet is the one who gives off the high, humming sound!* Now this high, humming sound, this perceptiveness and sensitivity, is partly what he was born with and partly what he maintains, often at the expense of a good deal else. No poet comes out of a poem the same person he was when he went in. Writing poetry is a reciprocal act in which one re-creates experience and oneself. One good reason why in poetry one cannot afford to be imprecise, or cheap, or shoddy, or dishonest. It will all come home to roost.

*From *Writing Poetry*, by John Holmes: The Writer, Inc., Boston, Massachusetts, 1960.

In short, I believe there is no dichotomy between the creative imagination and reality. Quite the contrary. I think that man is constantly trying to bring down into the world of time the essences of what he dimly but intuitively feels is timeless. One of the ways in which he tries is through poetry. Without poetry, a certain kind of Reality is speechless. Or to put it a slightly different way, I believe that we inhabit two worlds at once, the world of time and the world of timelessness, and that poetry is a bridge that lets us cross over.

Poetry gives us the present embedded in eternity. This is not far from saying that poetry is one way of experiencing "the eternal Now" of which the mystics speak. Poetry is the swift language of the intuition, as prose is the slower language of the intellect. And through poetry one reaches toward what man has always reached toward: order, unity, a kind of suprasymmetry. And beyond even this, toward stars that have not yet begun to show their light. In this kind of knowing is happiness and sometimes rapture. It is a timeless pilgrimage, with its ends forever origins. For it is not knowledge that spells a final answer, but rather knowledge that goes on to ask the more perilous question.

DATE DUE

GAYLORD			PRINTED IN U.S A.